U0368646

1+X实用英语交际职业技能实训工作手册（初级）

主编 肖 勇

副主编 刘国平 严眹芳 张源晴 杨 琨

清华大学出版社
北京

内 容 简 介

本书适应国家职业教育 1+X 证书考试要求，以《实用英语交际职业技能等级标准（初级）》为依据，从职业院校学生英语实际水平与能力出发，侧重英语基础知识训练，强化学生必备的词汇、语法知识和能力，书中设计了大量的词汇训练与英语交际活动任务，培养学习者实用英语交际职业能力。本书注重学用一体、学练结合，注重在学习活动中提升学习者对行业、企业基本业务和传统文化的认知，为学习者毕业后服务涉外企业打下扎实的基础。

本书适合中等职业学校高年级、高等职业学校低年级的学生以及参加实用英语交际职业技能等级证书（初级）考试的社会人士。

图书在版编目（CIP）数据

1+X 实用英语交际职业技能实训工作手册：初级 / 肖勇主编 . — 北京：清华大学出版社，2024.5
ISBN 978-7-302-66080-4

Ⅰ . ① 1… Ⅱ . ① 肖… Ⅲ . ① 英语－等级考试－自学参考资料 Ⅳ . ① H310.42

中国国家版本馆 CIP 数据核字（2024）第 072579 号

责任编辑：雷　桢
封面设计：傅瑞学
责任校对：刘　静
责任印制：沈　露

出版发行：清华大学出版社
　　　　网　　　址：https://www.tup.com.cn，https://www.wqxuetang.com
　　　　地　　　址：北京清华大学学研大厦A座　　　　邮　　编：100084
　　　　社 总 机：010-83470000　　　　邮　　购：010-62786544
　　　　投稿与读者服务：010-62776969，c-service@tup. tsinghua. edu. cn
　　　　质量反馈：010-62772015，zhiliang@tup. tsinghua. edu. cn
印 装 者：三河市铭诚印务有限公司
经　　销：全国新华书店
开　　本：185mm×260mm　　　　印　　张：8.5　　　　字　　数：193 千字
版　　次：2024 年 7 月第 1 版　　　　印　　次：2024 年 7 月第 1 次印刷
定　　价：39.50 元

产品编号：102993-01

前 言
Preface

编写背景

实用英语交际职业技能等级证书（Vocational English Test System，VETS），是教育部职业技术教育中心研究所授权发布的职业技能等级证书。VETS 等级证书考查和认定职业教育在校生、毕业生和社会人员在职场使用英语完成工作的技能水平，旨在为国家和社会培养符合时代需求的高素质国际化复合型技术技能人才。2020 年 12 月，VETS 被正式纳入 1+X 证书制度试点工作。VETS 考试包括初级、中级、高级三个级别，促使职业教育在校生、毕业生和社会人员提升英语交际职业技能。

为了帮助 VETS 学习者学习 VETS 相关课程及备考，我们编写了《1+X 实用英语交际职业技能实训工作手册（初级）》。本书凝聚编者团队多年的 VETS 教学培训和考试辅导经验，针对高职高专 VETS 学习者的特点及薄弱环节，编写对应的实训练习，有针对性地提升学习者的语言能力、应试能力和英语实际运用能力，为学习者学习 VETS 和备考打下扎实的基础。

教材特色

1. 填补VETS实训教材空白

目前，VETS 相关配套教材主要满足课堂教学需要，理论篇幅占比过多，实训案例较少，一个模块仅提供一个案例用于课堂展示。由于没有配套实训教材，学习者缺乏具体情境下的参照案例，实训实操难以有效开展，整个教学中理论多、实训少，因此实际学习效果不佳。本书有力填补了 VETS 实训教材的空白。一方面，有助于丰富学习者在对外贸易场景下的工作经验；另一方面，案例实操有助于提升学习者的职场英语技能，与未来职场无缝对接。

2. 体现涉外行业特色

本书基于涉外企业特定需求，注重提升学习者对涉外行业、企业基本业务和传统文化的认知，有助于提升学习者对企业的融入感和体验感，为学生毕业后服务涉外企业打下扎实基础。本书将涉外企业一般日常事务的典型领域细化为具体工作任务，以适合学习者实训、促进学习者技能提升为目标，可用于学习者课后实操与练习。书中的实训任务贴合真实的职场工作场景，学习者可通过完成口、笔头报告，项目书，电子邮件等多样化的任务，以现场演讲、视频、音频、作品等各种形式展现学习效果。

3. 强化语言形式的学习

本书基于高职高专学习者英语基础薄弱的情况，强化语言教学，设计大量词汇训练，夯实学习者英语语言基础与能力，帮助学习者提升涉外职场语言应用能力。

4. 贯彻新发展理念，融入中国传统文化教育

党的二十大报告中指出，推动战略性新兴产业融合集群发展，全面推进乡村振兴，坚持中国特色社会主义文化发展道路，增强文化自信。本书在 Scenario 部分介绍了新能源、新材料、现代服务业等行业发展与趋势，助力学习者用英语讲好中国故事。书中设计了 Ancient Chinese Wisdom 模块，展示与单元内容相关的中华思想文化术语，弘扬中华优秀传统文化，坚守中华文化立场，坚定文化自信，发挥外语学习融通中外文化、增进文明交流的优势，助力学生用英语讲好中国故事，传播好中国声音。

编者在编写过程中得到了宜春职业技术学院领导、教务处和师范学院领导的大力支持，相关教师对教材编写也提出了很多中肯的意见和建议，在此向他们表示衷心的感谢。

由于编者水平有限，时间仓促，书中疏漏之处在所难免，欢迎各位专家与同仁不吝赐教。

编者
2024 年 5 月

教学建议
Suggestions for teaching materials

　　本书针对高职高专学生英语实际水平，强化语言知识学习。书中设计丰富的词汇练习，通过多样化的词汇操练、巩固练习，侧重夯实高职高专学生的英语语言基本功。同时，本书关注时代热点，书中选用真实的案例，通过大量案例实训、实操，提升学生在职场上的英语交际能力；还结合中华传统思想教育，把语言教育与人文教育有机结合。

教材结构与教学建议

　　每个单元包括 7 个模块的学习与实训内容，教师根据教学进度与实际需要，可将相关素材用于课堂中练习，也可作为课后实训任务。

　　行业展望：关注新能源汽车、绿色发展、企业创新、国际贸易等新兴行业、热点话题的发展及讨论，拓展学生行业视野。

　　单元任务：明确本单元学习目标、学习内容及职场任务。

　　词汇训练：针对高职高专学生英语学习规律与英语学习难点，补充、设计大量词汇操练题。

　　典型案例：结合具体行业，提供丰富的职场典型案例，帮助学生熟悉行业典型工作任务。

　　案例实训：参考 VETS 考试题型，补充职场案例，为学生实训实操及 VETS 备考提供场景与素材。

　　思想探讨：选用与本单元主题相关的中华思想文化术语，开展主题探讨，助力学生用英语讲好中国故事。

　　拓展阅读：补充与本单元主题或相关行业相近的阅读语篇，在扩大学生知识面的同时，提升学生的英语阅读能力。

目 录
Contents

Unit 1 Announce a Team Building Event

||| Scenario

● Industry Outlook

China is committed to developing friendly and cooperative relations with all countries based on the Five Principles of Peaceful Coexistence. We will promote the construction of a new type of international relations, deepen global partnerships featuring equality, openness, and cooperation, and foster coordination and sound interactions among major countries to establish a pattern of peaceful coexistence, overall stability, and balanced development.

The development of new energy enterprises in Yichun City, Jiangxi Province, is currently undergoing rapid changes. With the support of the government and the efforts of a large number of new energy companies, Yichun is striving to become a leader in the global energy industry. In particular, the renewable energy industry has experienced tremendous growth in Yichun. Furthermore, Yichun's new energy companies are also developing in other areas such as energy storage technology and biofuel production. The leading companies in these areas in the city are setting industry standards and creating jobs for local people. The government is also supporting the development of new energy enterprises in Yichun by providing financing support, planning and allocating land resources, as well as creating a conducive business environment. These efforts have helped attract more investment and innovation to the city. Overall, Yichun's new energy industry is showing strong development and is poised to become a global leader in the field. The government's support and the efforts of new energy companies have played a crucial role in this progress.

The organization of team building activities for companies is significant. Such activities bring people together to work towards a common goal, fostering a sense of belonging and teamwork, which promotes a positive work environment. They also provide an opportunity to share ideas, challenge each other's ideas, and develop new strategies. Furthermore, team building activities can improve team members' creativity and problem-solving abilities.

Given the opportunity to collaborate on complex problems, team members can develop a stronger sense of responsibility and accountability while also learning from each other's strengths and weaknesses. By attracting qualified individuals to join your team and helping them become more efficient and successful through training and collaboration, you can build stronger relationships with your colleagues and clients, ultimately yielding better business outcomes. Therefore, organizing team building activities for corporate teams is an essential component of any successful business organization. This allows you to promote effective communication, cooperation, learning and innovation within your team.

An announcement is a public or official statement that gives people some information about an event, which usually covers the time, place, participants and arrangement. There are two kinds of announcements, namely the written and the oral. Compared with a written one, an oral announcement is less formal.

Words, Phrases and Sentences

Words and phrases concerning team building.

1. Translate the following words and phrases into Chinese or English.

○ **Team**

strengthen team spirit　　＿＿＿＿＿＿＿＿＿＿＿

national team　　＿＿＿＿＿＿＿＿＿＿＿

investigating team　　＿＿＿＿＿＿＿＿＿＿＿

行政部　　＿＿＿＿＿＿＿＿＿＿＿

互助组　　＿＿＿＿＿＿＿＿＿＿＿

队长　　＿＿＿＿＿＿＿＿＿＿＿

○ **Announcement**

meeting announcement　　＿＿＿＿＿＿＿＿＿＿＿

announce results　　＿＿＿＿＿＿＿＿＿＿＿

public announcement　　＿＿＿＿＿＿＿＿＿＿＿

奖项公布　　＿＿＿＿＿＿＿＿＿＿＿

口头通知　　＿＿＿＿＿＿＿＿＿＿＿

发布通知 _____

○ **Cooperation**

cultural cooperation _____

cooperative efforts _____

mutual cooperation _____

加强合作 _____

国际合作 _____

紧密合作 _____

2. Translate the following phrases into Chinese.

(1) team building activities _____

(2) establish team goals _____

(3) physical fitness _____

(4) goal setting _____

(5) team members _____

(6) team goal _____

(7) misunderstanding _____

(8) future cooperation _____

(9) travel agency _____

(10) significant event _____

3. Translate the following phrases into English.

(1) 新员工 _____

(2) 加强交流 _____

(3) 极好的机会 _____

(4) 相互了解 _____

(5) 每周例会 _____

(6) 做好充分准备 _____

(7) 总经理 _____

(8) 做最终决定 _____

(9) 与时俱进 _____

(10) 回头再找你 _____

4. Find the words or phrases in the text with the meanings below and write them on the lines.

(1) _____ attention and management implying responsibility for safety

(2) _____ more distant especially in degree

(3) _____ to ask sb. in a friendly way to do sth.

(4) _____ to become more focused on an area of activity or field of study

(5) _____ the state of serving as an official and authorized delegate or agent

(6) _____ a small part that can be considered separately from the whole

(7) _____ to put sb. to work for you

(8) _____ to make sth. strong or stronger

(9) _____ a time when a particular situation makes it possible to do or achieve sth.

(10) _____ to tell people sth. officially, especially about a decision, plans, etc.

5. Complete the following sentences by filling in each blank with an appropriate word or phrase from the box below. Change its form if necessary.

participate	split	multi-function hall	treasure	relax
schedule	reflect	performance	invite	charge

(1) There is an around 500-square-meter _____ and two conference rooms for all kinds of meetings and banquets.

(2) I'm going to spend the weekend just _____ .

(3) His leg injury prevented active _____ in any sports.

(4) Send it to whoever is in _____ of sales.

(5) The new meeting room has been finished one weeks ahead of _____ .

(6) It was an impressive _____ by the Chinese team.

(7) We were _____ up into groups to discuss the question.

(8) I _____ his friendship.

(9) Before I decide, I need time to _____ .

(10) It was a great honour to be _____ here today.

6. Fill in the blanks with appropriate words.

(1) Ladies and gentleman, please allow me to _____（发布通知）.

(2) It will be a _____（良机）to get to know each other.

(3) First, the event will be held in the _____（多功能厅）.

(4) An agency _____（专门从事）team building will be _____（负责）this event.

(5) We will return at 4:30 p.m. and then a party will be held at night, which will feature a buffet and some _____（现场表演）.

7. Translate the following sentences into English.

(1) 此项活动有利于培养团队精神。

_____

(2) 为了让大家相互增进了解，公司决定组织一次团建活动。

_____

(3) 每个团队大概有 5 ～ 6 名成员。

_____

(4) 最后由队长总结本队成员表现。

_____

(5) 所有参与者将会获得一些小礼物。

Reading

I

In "Fulfill the task", you will be asked to describe how to write a good oral announcement for a company's team building activity. The announcement should include the following elements.

1. Opening (call for the attention of audience).

2. Brief description of the team building event.

3. Time and location of the event (e.g., start time, end time, and location, etc.).

4. Specific activities planned for the event (such as team bonding activities, group discussions, and physical fitness exercises, etc.).

5. Benefits of the event (such as improving team collaboration, fostering team spirit, and enhancing employee motivation, etc.).

6. Contact information for the event organizer (e.g., name, phone number, email address, etc.).

7. Note and gratitude to the listeners (such as looking forward to their active participation in the upcoming team building activities).

During your writing practice, you should pay close attention to the above elements and provide sufficient details to ensure that the announcement is concise yet informative, easy for employees to understand, and makes sense from a strategic communication perspective. Additionally, it is important to avoid using offensive or negative language that could be misinterpreted by employees.

Finally, it is important to emphasize that the written announcement should be objective and reliable, rather than trying to manipulate the information to gain a desired effect. Please always approach your writing exercise with honesty and a concern for employee well-being.

II

Please pay close attention, new hires!

Great news has arrived for you! On Friday, our company is hosting a team-building activity at the community sports complex. Although the specifics of the activity are still private, we can guarantee that it will be both enjoyable and demanding.

The event begins at 6 p.m. and lasts for almost three hours. We will be joined by a member of the company leadership and an HR representative. You will have an opportunity to work with your coworkers and develop your communication skills while participating in a variety of challenges and activities.

Recently, we have all worked really hard to ensure the prosperity of our organization. It's finally time to unwind and reconnect with one another. The team building event will allow you to develop your relationship and become more social.

We hope you will all be able to attend the event. Please let us know if there are any changes or if you wish to participate in the event.

Please mark your calendars and get ready for a fun-filled day!

▌ Task

Suppose you are Li Ning, a secretary of general manager at New Era Lithium Technology Co., Ltd.. Your company is going to organize a team building event at the weekend. Now you are going to make an announcement to the new staff on Wednesday.

The Team Building Event	
Time	10:00 a.m. – 9:00 p.m., Sunday, September 10th
Place	Sports center
Participants	The new staff
Activities	Just one lie, blind and dumb, treasure hunt, etc.
Meals	Buffet in the dining hall

Now complete the announcement according to the information provided.

Dear all,

    May I have your attention please? I'm Li Ning, the secretary of general manager. (1) _____ . In order to get to know each other better and build on our team spirit, our company has decided to (2) _____ on September 10th. At this event, we'll meet outside our company at the front door and take a bus to (3) _____ at 10 a.m.. We have organized (4) _____ there. We will return at 9 p.m. and then a party will be held at night, which will provide a buffet and some live performances. If you are willing to join this event, please contact me by this Friday. I hope you will enjoy it! (5) _____ .

Ancient Chinese Wisdom

Read the following quotes and answer the questions below.

Triumph Comes When Leaders and Followers Share the Same Goal（上下同欲者胜）

Therefore, there are five ways to know how to win: those who know whether they can fight or not, those who know how to use a few, those who share the same desires, those who treat others with caution, and those who are able to resist the ruler. (*Attack by Stratagem, Master Sun's Art of War*)

故知胜有五：知可以战与不可以战者胜，识众寡之用者胜，上下同欲者胜，以虞待不虞者胜，将能而君不御者胜。(《孙子兵法·谋攻篇》)

(**Notes:** Only by working together can we achieve victory. Anyone, regardless of their position, should hold the same aspirations, willpower, and goals, so as to gather the wisdom of everyone and maximize their combat effectiveness.)

1. Unity or competition, which is more important in work? Why?

_____

2. How do you unite colleagues in work to improve your work efficiency?

_____

Extended Reading

Team building is an essential aspect of any successful organization or enterprise. It refers to the process of enhancing the interpersonal relationships, communication, trust, and understanding among members of a group or team with the aim of achieving a common goal or set of objectives. Team building activities help bring people together, break the ice, and establish a perceived sense of community among team members. The following passage provides an overview of team building and its importance in various contexts, with examples of activities that can help strengthen team bonds.

First and foremost, team building activities help improve communication within a group. When people work in a team, it is vital that they communicate effectively to achieve the objectives of the team. Team building activities provide a relaxed and fun environment for team members to open up and express their thoughts and opinions. Additionally, team building activities also help improve listening skills. When people are given the opportunity to express their ideas, they also become more attentive and interested in what other team members have to say.

Moreover, team building activities foster trust among team members. Trust is essential in any relationship, especially in a work setting where people are expected to rely on each other for support and guidance. Team building activities designed to foster trust commonly involve tasks that require collaboration or mutual support, such as rope courses, trust falls, or group survival courses. These activities help team members understand that they can trust one another and rely on each other together success.

Furthermore, team building activities encourage autonomy and creativity. When people work in a team, it is essential that they are able to think outside the box and suggest innovative ideas to achieve the team's goals. Team building activities that encourage brainstorming, idea generation, and critical thinking help foster creativity and can lead to better outcomes for the team.

Finally, team building activities help teams identify and address issues quickly. In any team setting, there may be issues or conflicts that need to be addressed. Team building activities provide an opportunity for team members to open up and discuss issues or conflicts they may have with other team members or the direction of the team. This opportunity helps teams identify any potential weaknesses or issues that may be affecting their performance and allows them to address these issues quickly together success.

In conclusion, team building is essential for any team or organization that wants to achieve success. It enhances communication, fosters trust and mutual support, encourages creativity and critical thinking, and identifies issues quickly and efficiently. Team members who work together effectively are more likely to achieve the team's goals and create a sense of community and camaraderie within the team. Therefore, organizations should invest in regular team building activities to ensure that their teams remain cohesive and productive.

(   ) 1. Which is NOT the main purpose of team building?

    A. To improve communication.

    B. To foster trust.

    C. To encourage creativity.

    D. To have fun.

(   ) 2. What is the benefit of team building activities in improving communication?

    A. They provide a relaxed environment for team members to open up and express their thoughts and opinions.

    B. They help team members understand that they can trust one another.

    C. They encourage team members to work together and generate innovative ideas.

    D. They help team members to quickly and efficiently address any issues or conflicts.

(   ) 3. What is the essential aspect of team building activities mentioned in the passage?

    A. The process of enhancing communication, trust, and understanding among team members.

    B. The use of rope courses, trust falls, and group survival courses.

    C. The common objective or set of objectives to be achieved by the team.

    D. The number of people participating in the activities.

(   ) 4. What is the benefit of team building activities in fostering trust among team members?

        A. They help team members understand that they can trust each other and rely on each other for support and guidance.

        B. They encourage team members to work together and generate innovative ideas.

        C. They help team members to quickly and efficiently address any issues or conflicts.

        D. They enhance communication within a group.

(   ) 5. What is the benefit of team building activities in encouraging creativity and critical thinking?

        A. They help teams to achieve their goals by generating new ideas and innovative solutions.

        B. They help teams to identify any issues or conflicts that need to be addressed quickly and efficiently.

        C. They help teams to work together more effectively and achieve better outcomes for the team.

        D. They provide an opportunity for team members to open up and discuss any issues or conflicts they may have with other team members or the direction of the team.

Unit 2 Write a Hotel Reservation Email

● **Industry Outlook**

China's Belt and Road Initiative (BRI) （一带一路）is a strategy aiming to connect Europe, Asia and Africa via land and sea. The goal is to improve integration, increase trade and improve economic growth. It was inspired by the Silk Road from the Han Dynasty 2,000 years ago which was an ancient network of trade routes that connected China to Europe through Eurasia for centuries.

The BRI comprises a Silk Road Economic Belt—a trans-continental passage that links China with Southeast Asia, South Asia, Central Asia, Russia and Europe by land—and a 21st century Maritime Silk Road, a sea route connecting China's coastal regions with Southeast and South Asia, the South Pacific, the Middle East and Eastern Africa, all the way to Europe.

More than 2,000 years ago, traditional Chinese medicine began to be communicated and promoted along the ancient Silk Road in countries along the route, becoming an important part of Sino-foreign trade exchanges. Now, with the change of health concept and medical model, the exchange and cooperation in terms of traditional Chinese medicine have become a new highlight of the high-quality development of the the Belt and Road Initiative.

Yichun Youren Chinese Herb Co., Ltd. is a modern Chinese medicine enterprise which covers the cultivation of medicinal materials, the processing of Chinese herbal medicine decoction pieces, the manufacture of Chinese patent medicines, product research and development, as well as import and export trade.

In order to better promote traditional Chinese medicine into the international market, participating in international exhibitions and holding meetings are common practices of the company. In order to organize meetings, we need to be able to write hotel reservation emails.

A letter of hotel reservation is one that is sent to reserve a place, such as a conference, function, or activity in a hotel. The reservation letter generally includes the number and type of the rooms, the arrival and departure dates, the length of stay, facility requirement, meals, recreational facilities and other preferences.

Words, Phrases and Sentences

Words and phrases concerning reservation emails.

1. Translate the following words and phrases into Chinese or English.

○ **Reserve**

make a reservation   _____

reserve seats   _____

reserve tickets   _____

订个房间   _____

确定预订订单   _____

取消预订   _____

○ **Attend**

attend a reception   _____

attend a trade fair   _____

attend a dinner party   _____

参加会议   _____

与会者   _____

参加研讨会   _____

○ **Confirm**

confirm check-in time   _____

an order confirmation email   _____

confirm room type   _____

确认订单   _____

确认预订   _____

确认离店时间   _____

2. Translate the following phrases into Chinese.

(1) room type   _____

(2) room rate   _____

(3) buffet breakfast   _____

(4) cardholder   _____

(5) credit card   _____

(6) length of stay   _____

(7) arrival date   _____

(8) departure date   _____

(9) 5-star accommodation   _____

(10) tourist attractions   _____

(11) set meal   _____

(12) a seating capacity   _____

(13) informal workshop   _____

(14) vegetarian set menu   _____

(15) make an appointment   _____

3. Translate the following phrases into English.

(1) 入住   _____

(2) 退房   _____

(3) 单间   _____

(4) 大床房   _____

(5) 双人间   _____

(6) 跨境电子商务   _____

(7) 年会   _____

(8) 贸易协会   _____

(9) 行政部主任   _____

(10) 营销策略   _____

4. Find the words or phrases in the text with the meanings below and write them on the lines.

(1) _____ to spread over the area mentioned

(2) _____ the money that is available to a person or an organization and a plan of how it will be spent over a period of time

(3) _____ a room or hall with equipment for doing physical exercise, for example, in a school

(4) _____ a piece of equipment for projecting photographs or films/

movies onto a screen

(5) _____ the opportunity or right to use sth. or to see sb./sth.

(6) _____ to prepare sb. for an activity or task, especially by teaching them what they need to know

(7) _____ buildings, services, equipment, etc. that are provided for a particular purpose

(8) _____ occurring once a year

(9) _____ to ask for a seat, table, room, etc. to be available for you or sb. else at a future time

(10) _____ a person who does not eat meat or fish

5. Complete the following sentences by filling in each blank with an appropriate word or phrase from the box below. Change its form if necessary.

budget	delivery	payment	order	access
reserve	cover	equip	gym	projector

(1) Everyone should enjoy the right of _____ to the public library.

(2) The company needs to balance the _____ each year.

(3) I usually go to the _____ after my supper.

(4) A _____ is a machine that projects films or slides onto a screen or wall.

(5) Each conference room is _____ with a screen, flip-chart and projector.

(6) Water _____ a large proportion of the earth's surface.

(7) We'll _____ the ticket for you till tomorrow noon.

(8) For the convenience of elderly people receiving goods, we offer customers a free home _____ service.

(9) The husband lost his job and they were finding it difficult to meet the _____ on their car.

(10) I would like to place an _____ for ten copies of this book.

6. Fill in the blanks with appropriate words.

(1) I would like to _____（预订）a single room that contains a bathroom and three double rooms, each of which contains a bathroom.

(2) We look forward to _____（到达）at your hotel around 16:00 on September 13th.

(3) Thank you for your time, and look forward to your _____（回复）.

(4) I am writing to _____（确认）the details of the reservation I would like to make at East Hotel after speaking with Sam Gordon on April 1st last week.

(5) We have a few special _____（要求）as follows.

7. Translate the following sentences into English.

(1) 为满足你的条件，我推荐 Hill Hotel。

(2) 如果你们还有其他疑问，请告诉我。

_____

(3) 餐费在我们的预算之内。

_____

(4) 酒店总经理确认了房间预订。

_____

(5) 请回复确认我的预订。

_____

 **Reading**

I

How to write a hotel reservation email

In most cases, we can book hotels through apps. Online booking is the most popular, because it's easy to call the hotel and tell the staff what you need. However, sometimes we need to book hotels through emails, especially when traveling abroad. We also reserve hotel venues for large-scale business-related events. Learning to write a good hotel reservation is one of the daily businesses of many large companies.

A well-written email will leave a positive impression and being polite, clear, and specific in your email will help the hotel staff understand your requirements and assist you promptly. A hotel reservation email should include the following information.

1. Subject line: Use a subject line like "Hotel Reservation Request" to indicate your intention clearly.

2. Greeting: Start your email with a polite and professional greeting, addressing the hotel.

3. Introduce yourself: Briefly introduce yourself and mention the purpose of your email, which is to inquire about the availability and make a reservation.

4. Dates and room details: Clearly state the dates of your intended stay and specify the type and number of rooms you require.

5. Request information: Ask for specific details, such as room rates, applicable discounts, amenities, and reservation policies. This will ensure you have all necessary information before confirming your reservation.

6. Special preferences or requests: If you have any preferences or special requests, such as a non-smoking room or a room with a view, kindly mention them in your email.

7. Polite language: Use polite language throughout your email, expressing your appreciation and gratitude for their assistance.

8. Contact information: Include your full name and contact details (email address and phone number) so that the hotel can easily reach you to confirm the reservation.

9. Closing: Thank the hotel for their attention and express your anticipation of their prompt response. Sign off with a professional closing, such as "Best regards" or "Sincerely".

Ⅱ

From: John Liu @123.com

To: Xie Da@163.com

Subject: hotel confirmation

Dear sir,

I am writing this letter to you to reserve rooms for our company guests from January 1st to January 10th with breakfast, lunch, and dinner services in your hotel. I need three double rooms with Wi-Fi and room services. The rooms should be cleaned and airy. Kindly share the available room details with the rates and payment modes. I am informing you of this a month before to avoid any inconvenience. I will be grateful to you.

Sincerely Yours,

John Liu

Read the letter and answer the following questions.

1. What kind of letter is this?

_____

2. What did John Liu reserve in his letter?

_____

3. How long will Liu's guests stay in the hotel?

_____

 Task

Suppose you are Sam Liu, an adminitrative manager at Yichun Youren Chinese Herb Co., Ltd.. Your company is going to hold the annual business meeting, and you are asked to reserve a meeting hall at Yichun Yingbinguan Hotel. Now you are going to write a reservation email to Wang Hui, the marketing manager of the hotel.

The Annual Business Meeting	
Time	9:30 a.m. – 6:00 p.m. March 1st
Rooms	10 double rooms and 2 single rooms
Meals	set meals for 100 attendants
Other equipment	projector to show a video clip

Now complete the reservation email according to the information provided.

From: Sam Liu@hotmail.com

To: Hui Wang@hotmail.com

Subject: Reserve a meeting hall

Dear Ms. Wang

    I'm Sam Liu, from Yichun Youren Chinese Herb Co., Ltd. (1) _____ _____ from 9:30 a.m. to 6:00 p.m. on March 1st, and I'm writing to make a reservation for a meeting hall at your hotel.

    We have a few requirements as follows.

    (2) _____ to show a video clip.

    (3) _____ , and we'd like to order set meals for them. 22 attendants will be staying overnight, so (4) _____ .

    Please (5) _____ by replying to this email.

Best wishes,

Sam Liu

Ⅲ Ancient Chinese Wisdom

Read the following quote and answer the questions below.

A Craftsman Must Sharpen His Tools to Do His Job（工欲善其事，必先利其器）

Confucius said," A craftsman must sharpen his tools to do his job. When you are in a state, you should serve its capable officials and befriend the virtuous people." (*The Analects*)

子曰：“工欲善其事，必先利其器。居是邦也，事其大夫之贤者，友其士之仁者。”（《论语》）

(**Notes:** To do something well, one needs to make preparations. When we do things, we must ensure that our skills are advanced and our preparations are sufficient. When you have a new goal or engage in a new job, be sure to put in effort, learn relevant theories, and accumulate relevant experience.)

    1. What method do you plan to use to learn English well?

_____

2. What preparations will you make to be a qualified foreign trade practitioners?

___

Extended Reading

The modern hotel industry

The modern development of hotels has revolutionized the way we travel and experience the world. With advancements in technology and an increasing focus on sustainability, the hotel industry has evolved significantly in recent years. One of trends is the rise of digital booking platforms, which have made it easier than ever for travelers to compare prices and find the best deals. This has led to increased competition among hotels, forcing them to constantly innovate and improve their offerings in order to stay competitive.

One of the most significant changes in the hotel industry has been the rise of technology. Today, hotels use various technologies to enhance the guest experience, such as keyless entry, smart rooms, and voice-activated assistants. These technologies not only make the stay more convenient but also provide hotels with valuable data on customer preferences. Additionally, hotels have started to embrace artificial intelligence and machine learning to improve efficiency and streamline operations.

Sustainability has become a top priority for the hotel industry, as it is crucial for the long-term survival of our planet. Many hotels are now implementing eco-friendly practices, such as using solar panels, reducing single-use plastics, and implementing energy-efficient systems. Some hotels are even going beyond these measures and adopting a fully sustainable approach to their operations, including zero-waste policies and carbon-neutral initiatives.

Another key aspect of modern hotel development is the focus on personalized experiences. To cater to the diverse needs of their guests, hotels are now offering a wide range of amenities and services, such as spas, fitness centers, and gourmet restaurants. Additionally, hotels are using data-driven insights to customize their offerings and provide a more personalized experience for their guests. This includes personalized room preferences, customized travel itineraries, and personalized recommendations based on individual interests.

The modern hotel industry also places a strong emphasis on design and aesthetics. hotels are now designed to be visually appealing and Instagram-worthy, with unique architecture and interior design. This not only creates a memorable experience for guests but also helps hotels stand out in a competitive market.

The modern hotel industry is increasingly focusing on the digital transformation of its operations. This includes the use of digital platforms for bookings, the implementation of chatbots and other digital solutions to streamline customer service, and the use of big data to analyze customer behavior and improve marketing strategies.

The modern development of hotels has transformed the travel experience, providing guests with more personalized, sustainable, and convenient options. As technology and sustainability continue to shape the industry, hotels will continue to evolve and adapt to meet the changing needs of their customers. The future of hotels looks bright, with innovative designs, cutting-edge technology, and a focus on sustainability that will provide travelers with an unparalleled experience.

(　　) 1. How does technology change the modern hotel industry?

A. Enhance the guest experience.

B. Provide hotels with valuable data on customer preferences.

C. Improve efficiency and streamline operations.

D. All of the above.

(　　) 2. Which is not the eco-friendly practice the hotels are now implementing?

A. Using solar panels.

B. Increasing single-use plastics.

C. Implementing energy-efficient systems.

D. Adopting a fully sustainable approach to their operations.

(　　) 3. How do the hotels provide a more personalized experience for their guests?

A. Offering spas, fitness centers, and gourmet restaurants.

B. Using data-driven insights to customize their offerings.

C. Making personalized recommendations based on individual interests.

D. All of the above.

(　　) 4. Which is not the trend of modern hotel industry?

A. Growing emphasis on sustainability.

B. Emphasis on eco-friendliness.

C. Increasingly focusing on the digital transformation of its operations.

D. Placing no emphasis on design and aesthetics.

(　　) 5. Which is not the mentioned as the new practise of modern hotel?

A. Digital booking platforms.

B. Implementation of chatbots to streamline customer service.

C. Keyless entry in the hotel.

D. Using single-use plastics.

Unit 3 Write a Quick Operation Guide

Industry Outlook

The report to the 20th National Congress of the Communist Party of China pointed out that innovation will remain at the heart of China's modernization drive. We must uphold fundamental principles and break new ground as we are engaged in an unprecedented great cause. Only by upholding fundamental principles can we avoid losing our way and making subversive mistakes, and only through innovation can we grasp and lead the times. Meanwhile, we should promote the digitization of education, building a learning society and a learning country with lifelong learning for all.

In the workplace, we need to know how to use office equipment. As technicians, we need to read product manuals, and write quick operation guides for colleagues. Therefore, company technicians must strengthen their learning, cultivate innovative awareness and ability, and keep up with the trend of the company's product development. The product line will continue to diversify, new products will be introduced, and there will be an increasing need for quick product operation guides as a result of New Era Lithium Technology Co., Ltd.'s ongoing development and expansion.

Business Task

Quick operation guides are important tools that provide the processes and practices for carrying out a particular activity or operation. They typically serve as a source of direction and instructions for technicians, engineers, or clients who must operate machinery. These user-friendly tools offer detailed instructions for carrying out frequent tasks and frequently combine texts, images, and diagrams to make them simpler to comprehend and implement. They have benefits including quickness, versatility, and simplicity to suit various operational conditions. They are intended to provide quick and easy access to information about how to utilize a product's basic features without the need to read lengthy user manuals. These guides are usually supplied with the product, but they can also be obtained online via the manufacturer's website or other digital platforms.

Overall, quick operation guides play an important role in ensuring that users can use a product effectively and efficiently, reducing the likelihood of confusion, frustration, or errors that may occur in the absence of proper instruction. To write a clear and efficient operation guide, we should know what information needs to be included in it and the kind of writing style to use.

Words, Phrases and Sentences

Words and phrases concerning operation guide.

1. Translate the following words and phrases into Chinese or English.

○ **Operation**

computer operation   _____

commercial operation   _____

operate by electricity   _____

操作指南   _____

操作投影仪   _____

技术操作   _____

○ **Guide**

consumer guide   _____

how-to guide   _____

practical guide   _____

旅游指南   _____

用户指南   _____

指导说明   _____

○ **Concise**

concise introduction   _____

concise edition   _____

concise design   _____

简明的指南 _____

简明描述 _____

简洁原则 _____

2. Translate the following phrases into Chinese.

(1) user manual _____

(2) operating system _____

(3) software Setup _____

(4) network configuration _____

(5) projection screen _____

(6) start the computer _____

(7) set up the scanner _____

(8) connect the router to the Internet _____

(9) smart home _____

(10) Bluetooth connection _____

3. Translate the following phrases into English.

(1) 崭新的会议室 _____

(2) 快速操作指南 _____

(3) 打开投影仪 _____

(4) 简洁易读 _____

(5) 把……表达清楚 _____

(6) 关闭投影仪 _____

(7) 相信我 _____

(8) 完成指南 _____

(9) 没问题 _____

(10) 帮我一把 _____

4. Find the words or phrases in the text with the meanings below and write them on the lines.

(1) _____ to send sth. to a screen

(2) _____ a conductor for transmitting electrical or optical signals or electric power

(3) _____ to obey rules, laws, etc.

(4) _____ any nonverbal action or gesture that encodes a message

(5) _____ cap used to keep lens free of dust when not in use

(6) _____ receptacle providing a place in a wiring system where current can be taken to run electrical devices

(7) _____ expressing much in few words

(8) _____ a process or series of acts especially of a practical or mechanical nature involved in a particular form of work

(9) _____ to stay the same; continue in a place, position, or situation

(10) _____ lengthen in time; extend in scope or range or area

5. Complete the following sentences by filling in each blank with an appropriate word or phrase from the box below. Change its form if necessary.

cord	project	remain	previous	plug
concise	procedure	extend	brand-new	signal

(1) Chinese village culture in new century provides _____ development opportunity.

(2) When you are in danger, the most important thing is to _____ calm.

(3) The host ran a long extension _____ out from the house and set up a screen and a projector.

(4) Careful maintenance can _____ the life of your car.

(5) Information about safety _____ is in the pocket in front of you.

(6) Do you have any _____ experience of this type of work?

(7) The images are _____ onto the screen.

(8) Just _____ it in and see what happens.

(9) All I get is a busy _____ when I dial his number.

(10) Be sure to make it clear and _____ and avoid long-windedness.

6. Fill in the blanks with appropriate words.

(1) Employees should be fully acquainted with _____（应急程序）.

(2) If this _____（确认信息）appears, click "yes".

(3) His _____（公众形象）is very different from the real person.

(4) It also has a larger screen and a port that lets users _____（接入）an HDTV.

(5) I knew that concentration was the _____（基本要求）for learning.

7. Translate the following sentences into English.

(1) 如果您需要关闭投影仪，请连续按两次遥控器上的电源键。

_____

(2) 我必须更换吹风机的插头。

_____

(3) 当系统启动时，电源指示灯就会闪烁红光或绿光。

_____

(4) 按这两个键就可以在屏幕上的文件之间进行切换。

_____

(5) 警告！继续该操作将导致数据丢失。

_____

I

The format of a quick operation guide varies depending on the type of equipment and the operator's skills. However, the following are some common elements that should be included in a quick operation guide.

1. Table of contents: A table of contents is used to organize the information in the guide. It should include the title, purpose, and important dates.

2. Section headings: Sections are used to divide the guide into different subsections and provide a clear organization to ensure logical progression of the instructions.

3. Prerequisites: Each step of the process needs to have its necessary prerequisites. These prerequisites should be clearly defined and identified in the guide.

4. Steps: The steps in the guide should be clearly defined and easy to understand. The order of steps should be logical and consistent with the overall flow of the task. Images are often used to illustrate the steps in the guide. Typical examples are used to demonstrate the steps in the guide and provide a practical example for reference. These examples should be consistent with the equipment or operation and easy to understand.

5. Warnings and precautions: Warnings and precautions are used to inform the reader of any potential risks or problems that may arise during the operation, including health and safety considerations. Key words are used to identify important safety precautions or warnings that need to be taken during the process. These precautions should be clearly identified and understood by the reader.

6. Codes and labels: Codes and labels are used to identify specific equipment or operations. These codes and labels should be consistent with the equipment or operations and easy to understand.

In writing a quick operation guide, it is important to ensure that the information is accurate, clear, and practical. It is also vital to ensure that the guide is easy to understand, organized, and practical for the reader. Finally, it is essential to ensure that the guide complies with relevant regulations and industry standards to ensure its legitimacy and reliability.

II
Quick Operation Guide for Printers

Introduction

Printers are a common kind of office equipment that allows us to print documents, pictures, and more. Although they are convenient, maintaining and operating a printer can be challenging. This guide will provide you with step-by-step instructions on how to maintain and operate your printer. We will cover topics such as basic setup, printing options, paper management, etc..

Basic Setup

1. Connect the printer to the computer by using a USB cable.

2. Plug one end of the power cable into the printer, and plug the other into an electrical outlet.

3. Press the power button of the printer.

4. Launch the printer setup program.

5. In the printer setup program, make sure that the printer is set according to correct settings and that the print queue is empty.

6. Open your documents, click the "Print" button of the application to start the printer.

Printing Options

1. Select the document to be printed. You can select multiple documents by holding down the "Ctrl" key and selecting multiple items.

2. Select the printer language. You can select from a variety of languages, such as English, Chinese, and Japanese.

3. Select the number of copies you want to print. You can select a single copy, or a batch of multiple copies.

4. Adjust the font size and color settings. You can increase or decrease the font size and color depth to improve printing quality.

Paper Management

1. Load the paper into the printer's carton, when you use the printer the first time.

2. Be patient until the paper is printed.

3. Clean up paper scraps. If the printer stops working during the printing process, check whether the printer is jammed.

Troubleshooting

1. If the printer is not printing, check the connection between the printer and computer. Make sure that the USB cable is properly connected and that there is no power loss in the computer.

2. If the print quality is poor, check the print settings in Windows or the printer setup program. You can try adjusting the print resolution, bit depth, or other settings until you find the desired output.

3. If problems persist, try connecting the printer to another computer or restart the printer to see if the problem is related to the hardware or software on that device.

Summary

This guide provides you with step-by-step instructions on how to maintain and operate your printer. By following these instructions, you can improve printing quality and efficiency, and ensure that your documents are printed accurately. We hope this guide helps you with your printer operation needs. If you have any questions or need help with other issues, feel free to contact our customer service department at 188×××××××.

▌▌▌ Task

Suppose you are Chen Tao, a technician of New Era Lithium Technology Co., Ltd.. Your company has bought some brand-new printers. Now you are going to write a quick operation guide for the following printer.

Now complete the operation guide according to the information provided.

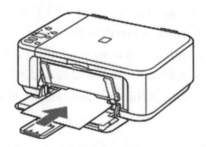

1. (1) _____ with the print side facing down.

2. (2) _____ and USB cable.

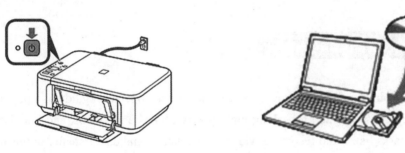

3. Press the (3) _____ .

4. Install (4) _____ on your computer.

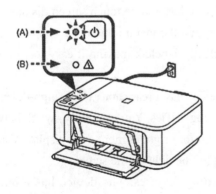

5. Check that (5) _____ green.

6. Find the "Print" function on your office software.

Ancient Chinese Wisdom

Read the following quote and answer the questions below.

Verification and Validation（效验）

In any discussion, if one contradicts the facts and does not use verification and validation, then no matter how lovely the contents or elaborate the arguments, no one will believe them. (Wang Chong: *A Comparative Study of Different Schools of Learning*)

凡论事者，违实不引效验，则虽甘义繁说，众不见信。（王充《论衡·知实》）

(**Notes:** Verification and validation is the only method or standard for determining the correctness of an argument. Whether or not an idea is correct cannot be determined solely by empty words or cleverness; rather, it has to be proved through "verification and validation".)

1. Is the quick operation guide just a simplification of the detailed product manual? Why?

_____

2. How do you make sure your product operation guide is exactly what the user needs?

_____

Extended Reading

Today, I'm going to show you how to quickly master the operation guide of a popular smart device. This device is designed for taking high-quality photos and videos, and it's also able to handle various tasks like audio recording, video conferencing, and data transfer. In this operation guide, we'll cover all the important functions and features of this device, so that you can start using it right away.

To begin with, we'll start with the basics. The device has a large touch screen display that's easy to use. You can swipe left or right to navigate through the menu options, or you can simply tap on an option to select it. The menu options are clearly labeled, making it easy to find what you need.

Next up, we'll cover the camera functions. The device has a rear camera with high-definition video recording capabilities, and a front camera for taking selfies. You can easily switch between the two cameras by tapping on the camera icon in the bottom right corner of the display. You can also adjust the focus and exposure settings by swiping left or right on the screen.

Following that, we'll explore the audio recording features. The device has a built-in microphone that's able to record high-quality audio. You can simply tap on the microphone icon in the bottom left corner of the display to start recording. You can also adjust the volume and other settings by navigating through the menu options.

Lastly, we'll cover the video conferencing capabilities of this device. It has a front-facing camera and a built-in speaker and microphone for video conferencing. You can simply tap on the video conferencing icon in the bottom right corner of the display to start a conference call. You can also adjust the volume and other settings by navigating through the menu options.

In conclusion, this is a popular smart device that's designed for taking high-quality photos and videos, and it's also able to handle various tasks like audio recording, video conferencing, and data transfer. In this operation guide, we've covered all of the important functions and features of this device, so that you can start using it right away. We hope that this operation guide will be helpful for you!

(　　) 1. What is the main function of this smart device?

      A. Taking high-quality photos and videos.

      B. Handling various tasks like audio recording.

      C. Video conferencing.

      D. Data transfer.

(　　) 2. How do you navigate through the menu options on the device's display?

      A. By swiping left or right.

      B. By tapping on the display.

      C. By pressing specific keys.

      D. By speaking commands.

(　　) 3. What is used for recording high-quality audio on the device?

      A. The rear camera.

      B. The front camera.

      C. The built-in microphone.

      D. The built-in speaker and microphone.

(　　) 4. What is the quickest way to start a video conference call on the device?

      A. By swiping left or right on the display.

      B. By tapping on the video conferencing icon in the bottom right corner of the display.

      C. By pressing a specific key on the keypad.

      D. By speaking a command to the device.

(　　) 5. Where can you find information about various functions and features of the device in the operation guide?

      A. In the menu options.

      B. In the user manual.

      C. In the help center.

      D. In the device's display settings.

Unit 4 Reply to Technical Enquiries

Industry Outlook

According to the Report of the 20th National Congress of the Communist Party of China, we should optimize the service reform, create a new system of highly effective service industries, offer refined services, and never forget that the Party's primary goal is to serve the people wholeheartedly.

Lithium resources are plentiful in the city of Yichun, Jiangxi province. There, the market for new energy products like lithium batteries and electric vehicles is booming. Technical support personnel are increasingly needed as new energy companies quickly upgrade their products.

Business Task

In business, after-sales service is an important part of the services enterprises offer. Providing good after-sales service helps to strengthen the brand image and develop brand loyalty. We need to know how to approach a customer who has technical enquiries and soft skills in basic communication are also necessary.

For people or companies, technical enquiry is a service that provides knowledgeable counsel on technological matters. Technical support is to assist clients in troubleshooting technology-related issues and offer them useful solutions to enhance their technical operations. Technical enquiry services have a broad range of topics that might be covered, including software creation, hardware selection, equipment operation and maintenance, and more. Technical consultants frequently have a wealth of knowledge and experience in their area of specialization, enabling them to provide specialized solutions that are suited to the requirements of their clients.

Technical enquiry services offer a wide range of advantages. Clients may benefit from expert guidance without having to spend more money on people or resources, prevent expensive technological failures, and feel more secure knowing that their technology is set up to meet their company goals. Technical enquiry services are frequently used by businesses to keep their operations running smoothly and effectively. Technical experts are frequently accessible 24/7 to provide clients with solutions when a need for technical assistance arises.

For businesses of all sizes looking to enhance their technical operations, technical enquiry services are essential.

Words, Phrases and Sentences

Words and phrases concerning technical enquiries.

1. Translate the following words and phrases into Chinese or English.

○ **Reply**

anonymous reply　　_____

make a reply　　_____

receive a reply　　_____

回复卡片　　_____

回复电子邮件　　_____

深思熟虑的回复　　_____

○ **Technical**

technical services　　_____

technical support　　_____

technical training　　_____

技术问题　　_____

信息技术　　_____

无线技术　　_____

○ **Enquiry**

technical enquiry　　_____

free enquiry service　　_____

enquiry system　　_____

查询软件　　_____

客户的咨询　　　　　　　　_____

查询和反馈　　　　　　　　_____

2. Translate the following phrases into Chinese.

(1) background enquiry　　　_____

(2) technical expert　　　　_____

(3) touch screen phone　　　_____

(4) model number　　　　　_____

(5) phone signal　　　　　　_____

(6) technical advancement　　_____

(7) technical error　　　　　_____

(8) secretarial enquiry　　　_____

(9) general enquiry　　　　　_____

(10) rechargeable battery　　_____

3. Translate the following phrases into English.

(1) 客服中心

(2) 技术问题　　　　　　　_____

(3) 智能手机

(4) 待机时间　　　　　　　_____

(5) 手机型号　　　　　　　_____

(6) 查看网站　　　　　　　_____

(7) 不管　　　　　　　　　_____

(8) 第四型号　　　　　　　_____

(9) 处理问题　　　　　　　_____

(10) 给他们回电话　　　　　_____

4. Find the words or phrases in the text with the meanings below and write them on the lines.

(1) _____ bright; gorgeous or prominent

(2) _____ remove the occupants

(3) _____ an expert who gives advice

(4) _____ not suitable or right or appropriate

(5) _____ to bring to the latest state of technology

(6) _____ a device that produces electricity

(7) _____ to empty sth. accomplished by allowing liquid to run out of it

(8) _____ a search for knowledge

(9) _____ a person engaged in one of the learned professions

(10) _____ bering approximately average or within certain limits in e.g. intelligence and development

5. Complete the following sentences by filling in each blank with an appropriate word or phrase from the box below. Change its form if necessary.

update	sensible	unstable	drain	professional
examination	brightness	improper	normal	notify

(1) The company invested much in the application research and development of high _____ LED in green lighting engineering.

(2) He had a third _____ and was declared unfit for duty.

(3) This bookcase is too _____ to hold so many books.

(4) Always seek _____ legal advice before entering into any agreement.

(5) Many of these problems can be minimized by _____ planning.

(6) Please _____ me of any change of address as soon as possible.

(7) Her face _____ of colour because of scare.

(8) He would never be _____ and he is always the perfect gentleman.

(9) The company has spent millions of RMB _____ their computer systems.

(10) Soon after, he received his acceptance letter from Jiangxi _____ University.

6. Fill in the blanks with appropriate words.

(1) I'd like to _____（预约）with Mr. Wang, the manager.

(2) Could you please _____（阐述技术原理）underlying your product's design?

(3) Could you please check the coding standards used in our system to _____ _____（遵守行业规则）.

(4) How often do you _____（遇见网络连接问题）, and how do you resolve them?

(5) In most instances we will _____（修好你的手机）within five working days.

7. Translate the following sentences into English.

(1) 这里的手机信号不好。

_____

(2) 感谢您的理解，您真的太贴心了。

_____

(3) 我很乐意为产品的任何后续问题提供帮助。

_____

(4) 可能是纸张受潮造成打印机卡纸。

_____

(5) 您的机子可能要返厂做进一步检查。

_____

I

When you respond to technical enquiries from customers, it is important to be professional, courteous, and thorough in your response. Here are some tips on how to effectively respond to customer enquiries.

1. Start by thanking the customers for their enquiry and letting them know that you understand their concern.

2. Ask the customers for more information if necessary to fully understand the issue they are experiencing.

3. Provide clear and concise information to address the customers' issues. Avoid using industry jargon or technical terms that the customers may not be familiar with.

4. Be patient and empathetic, as the customers may be frustrated or stressed due to the issue they are experiencing.

5. Offer solutions or suggestions to help the customers resolve their issue, and explain any steps they might need to take in order to carry out those solutions.

6. Encourage the customers to contact you again if they have any further questions or concerns.

7. Always end the conversation on a positive note by thanking the customers for their time and restating your commitment to providing excellent customer service.

II

Technician: Hello, this is Chen Tao, from New Era Lithium Technology Co., Ltd.. How may I help you today?

Mr. Johnson: Hi, I am Jim Johnson. I recently purchased one of your products and I am experiencing some issues with the battery. Can you help me out?

Technician: Sure, I would be happy to help you with that. Can you please provide me with some details about the issue you are facing?

Mr. Johnson: Well, the battery is not holding a charge for very long. It seems to drain very quickly.

Technician: Okay, I understand. Can you tell me the model number of the product you purchased?

Mr. Johnson: It's the ABC Model.

Technician: Thank you for providing that information. Based on what you are telling me, it seems the battery might be defective. Have you tried charging the battery for a longer period of time?

Mr. Johnson: Yes, I've tried that, but it still doesn't last very long.

Technician: Alright, have you tried a different charger to see if it makes any difference?

Mr. Johnson: No, I haven't tried that. Should I try that first?

Technician: Yes, that's a good idea. Sometimes the charger may not be properly charging the battery, which can lead to a reduction in the battery lifespan. If that doesn't work, then we may need to get the battery replaced.

Mr. Johnson: Okay, thank you for your suggestion. I'll try that out and see if it works.

Technician: You're welcome. If you have any further questions, feel free to give us a call anytime.

Mr. Johnson: Thanks a lot. I appreciate your help.

Technician: No problem at all. Have a great day.

Task

Suppose you are Fu Lei, a new technician of Better Life Co., Ltd.. You receive a call from Mr. Black, a customer who bought his personal computer from your company; however, his computer screen suddenly went black just now. You are going to reply to his questions.

Now complete the technical enquiry according to the information provided.

Fu: Hello, (1) _____ Better Life for help. This is Fu Lei. How can I help you?

Mr. Black: Hello? Can you help me? My computer! Oh man...

Fu: It's okay, sir, calm down. What happened?

Mr. Black: I turned on my laptop and it broke! I mean, (2) _____!

Fu: OK, sir. It sounds you might have a virus.

Mr. Black: I don't feel sick...let me check... Nope! No fever, I'm fine.

Fu: No, (3) _____ . I mean, it has a bad program on it. Maybe that's why it crashed. I recommend that (4) _____ in order to safely remove any unwanted spyware or trojans.

Mr. Black: Wait a minute, CRASH? Spyware? Trojans! What? Where? When?!

Fu: You open the antivirus software in your computer and then scan the whole disk with it. If you find any problems, the software will automatically deal with it; then you can check (5) __

_____ .

Mr. Black: OK, I'll try.

(A few minutes later...)

Mr. Black: The problem has been solved. Thank you very much. You are such a good person. Goodbye!

Fu: OK, I'm glad to help. Bye!

Read the following quote and answer the questions below.

Discerning Statements（知言）

If you do not discern statements of others, you cannot understand them. (*The Analects*)

不知言，无以知人也。(《论语》)

(**Notes:** In customer service, observation is crucial. By observing customers' language and behavior, we can better understand their needs and psychology, provide more accurate services, establish good customer relationships, and improve customer satisfaction and loyalty.)

1. How do you understand customers' needs and psychology through observing their language and behavior?

_____

2. How do you deal with customers' feedback and complaints through observing their language and behavior, and avoid complaints?

_____

Extended Reading

Dear Sir/Madam,

Thank you for your interest in our products and services. We are always delighted to receive enquiries from professionals and we appreciate the opportunity to answer any technical questions you may have.

1. What are the main features of your latest product?

Our latest product, model XYZ, is designed for maximum efficiency and ease of use. It has a sturdy metal body and a bright touchscreen interface that is simple to navigate. Additionally, XYZ has a range of pre-programmed functions that can be customised to meet specific user needs.

2. How does our product compare to competitors' products?

We take pride in the fact that our products are of the highest quality and durability, and are backed by an exceptional level of customer support. While our competitors may offer similar products, our main differentiator is our commitment to quality and customer satisfaction.

3. Can you provide a customised solution for our company?

Absolutely! We welcome the opportunity to discuss your company's unique needs and provide a customised solution. Our team of experts will work with you to design a product or service that meets your specific requirements.

4. What is your company's return policy?

We offer a 30-day return policy for unused items. However, we do not cover returns for items that have been partially used or damaged.

5. Are your products compliant with industry standards?

Yes, all of our products are designed to comply with industry standards. We regularly conduct various tests to ensure product compatibility in different industry standards. Furthermore, we also have a team of experts who are available to assist you with any product-specific standards compliance questions you may have.

We hope that these answers have been helpful. If you have any further questions or need assistance, please feel free to contact us at your convenience.

Thank you for your time and consideration.

Best regards,

Li Hua

(　　) 1. What is the main feature of the latest product?

      A. Its durability.

      B. Its sturdy metal body.

      C. The touchscreen interface.

      D. Pre-programmed functions.

(　　) 2. What is the return policy for unused items?

      A. 30-day return policy.

      B. 60-day return policy.

      C. 90-day return policy.

      D. 180-day return policy.

(　　) 3. Can customers get customised solutions?

      A. No.

      B. Yes.

(　　) 4. What is the difference between this product and competitors' products?

      A. Its durability.

      B. Its price.

      C. Its customer support.

      D. Its customisability.

(　　) 5. Are all of the company's products designed to comply with industry standards?

      A. Yes.

      B. No.

      C. Sometimes.

      D. It is unclear.

Unit 5 Make a Business Trip Itinerary

Scenario

Industry Outlook

Education, technology, and talent are the fundamental and strategic support for the comprehensive construction of a socialist modernized country. We must regard science and technology as our primary productive force, talent as our primary resource, and innovation as our primary driver of growth. Cultivating a large number of high-quality talents with both morality and talent is a long-term development plan for the country and the nation.

Strengthen international exchange of talents and make good use of various talents are effective policies to fulfil this long-term plan. J&K publications is a publishing house which conducts lots of international exchange every year. It has published a great many well-known books, helping readers from both home and abroad learn wisdom and knowledge from each other. Recently, it is going to launch a new book called *A Brief History of Chinese Royal Gardens* in Beijing. It has invited the writer, James Peter, to give a speech and communicate with the readers and other book writers at the book launch, and Lin Xi has been asked to make an itinerary for Professor Peter's visit to Beijing.

Business Task

Making a business trip itinerary is an important skill in business working environments, which is essential to leave a good impression to the business partner and boost the business ties between the two parties. A business trip itinerary usually includes five elements, which are date, time, event, place and note. If date, time or place is not determined, the letters "TBD" (to be determined) can be put wherever it is needed.

Words, Phrases and Sentences

Words and phrases concerning making a business trip itinerary.

1. Translate the following words and phrases into Chinese or English.

○ **Launch**

book launch _____

go to the launch _____

launch date _____

产品发布会 _____

发行最新的小说 _____

发射卫星 _____

○ **Arrange**

arrange an appointment _____

arrange for a car _____

arrange a book launch _____

安排会议 _____

安排一位员工 _____

安排出差 _____

○ **Itinerary**

a business trip itinerary _____

on the itinerary _____

make an itinerary _____

改变行程 _____

给经理看一下行程 _____

路线图 _____

2. Translate the following phrases into Chinese.

(1) against the clock _____

(2) book up _____

(3) postpone the visit _____

(4) advisory committee _____

(5) a tight schedule _____

(6) follow the itinerary map _____

(7) departure date _____

(8) on his arrival _____

(9) draft a business trip itinerary _____

(10) make a comparison _____

3. Translate the following phrases into English.

(1) 出版社

(2) 发行一本新书

(3) 转发一封邮件 _____

(4) 发表演讲 _____

(5) 核对行程 _____

(6) 直飞航班 _____

(7) 空出下午 _____

(8) 起草行程安排 _____

(9) 更合意的出行日期 _____

(10) 印象深刻 _____

4. Find the words or phrases in the text with the meanings below and write them on the lines.

(1) _____ the process of comparing two or more people or things

(2) _____ to make a product available to the public for the first time

(3) _____ a plane, train, etc. leaving a place at a particular time

(4) _____ to help sth. to happen or develop

(5) _____ to make sb. understand how important sth. is by emphasizing it

(6) _____ to write the first rough version of sth. such as a letter, speech or book

(7) _____ to produce a book, magazine, CD-ROM, etc, and sell it to the public

(8) _____ having won a prize

(9) _____ a plan of a journey, including the route and the places that you visit

(10) _____ a person who does not eat meat or fish

5. Complete the following sentences by filling in each blank with an appropriate word or phrase from the box below. Change its form if necessary.

impress	promote	draft	launch	comparison	departure

(1) Thomas Jefferson _____ the Declaration of Independence in 1776.

(2) Our CEO sincerely hopes to _____ cooperation between the two companies.

(3) It is said that the new Huawei smart phone will be _____ next year.

(4) They had received no news of him since his _____ from the country.

(5) I interviewed a number of candidates but none of them _____ me.

(6) The theme of his thesis is the _____ between Chinese and American cultures.

(7) The sales of the book can be _____ if the writer comes to the book launch.

(8) The beauty of Hangzhou leaves a good _____ to many foreign travelers.

(9) People always _____ public schools with private schools in terms of education.

(10) Professor Jane is going to _____ for London next Wednesday morning.

6. Fill in the blanks with appropriate words.

(1) The reception department is responsible to _____（安排住宿）for the participants of the book launch.

(2) I will _____（把他的邮件转发给你）to help you get more information about the meeting.

(3) Professor Lee wants to _____（去观光）after the book launch is over and the manager wants you to keep him company.

(4) Please _____（取得联系）if you have any questions about the products you have just purchased.

(5) Mr. James would like you to _____（安排行程）for Professor Lee's visit to Guangzhou next week.

7. Translate the following sentences into English.

(1) 我希望这个安排适合你。

_____

(2) 离开和到达的时间分别是什么？

_____

(3) 我们计划 7 月 15 日在东湖酒店举办一场新书发布会。

_____

(4) 约翰明天会到机场去接李教授。

_____

(5) 我很高兴能在这个活动上发表演讲。

_____

I

A business trip itinerary generally includes five basic elements: date, time, event, location, and postscripts. The date needs to be specific to a certain month, day, and day of the week. Time refers to the time of departure and return and the time of different arrangements. Specific matters include the main activities carried out during business travel. Location refers to the place where each activity is carried out and postscripts refer to the items that require special attention, such as contact information, accommodation information, transportation methods, weather conditions, and documents that need to be carried. When a business trip itinerary is arranged, it is important to pay attention to the following points.

1. Whether the task is general or important, it is necessary to obtain the business partner's consent before making the itinerary. Because business partners have their own work and life plans, if not communicated in a timely and effective manner, it may disrupt their work arrangements, and in severe cases, even disrupt the cooperation relationship between the two parties.

2. Leave room for it in terms of time. Many secretaries have made the mistake of arranging various matters extremely closely in order to race against the clock. This seems to be a tight schedule, as if one's potential has been fully utilized. However, it has been proven that this does not improve work efficiency at all.

3. Business itinerary arrangements require appropriate confidentiality. The schedule provided to other departments and drivers should not be too detailed, and only the copies provided to the secretary herself, relevant business partners and supervisors should be detailed. The more people know the detailed information of the schedule, the greater the likelihood of leakage, which is not conducive to the company's business development.

A business trip itinerary is usually a form, as it is simple and clear. Give one copy of the schedule to your supervisor, one copy to your business partner, keep one for yourself, and then make a copy to the relevant department and car driver. You should consider the following details in order to make a specific itinerary:

1. Determine the purpose and date of the business trip;

2. Confirm the business partner's business trip companion;

3. Book air tickets (pay attention to choosing the airline, aircraft type, and flight) and hotels (choose hotels that partners are accustomed to, and get familiar with hotel phone numbers, faxes, etc.);

4. Confirm pickup/drop-off personnel, and specify the contact information of the pickup/drop-off personnel;

5. Communicate with relevant personnel to determine a thoughtful schedule, including

breakfast, lunch, dinner arrangements, destination address, required travel time, reception personnel, location, attendees, events, agenda and other information.

II
Schedule

Date	Time	Topic	Location
March 30th, 2022.	08:00 – 08:15	Speech given by Dr. Allister Johnson, Sales Director in GM Company	Room 201
	08:15 – 08:30	Speech given by Xiao Yang, CEO of OPIAN Ltd.	Room 201
	08:30 – 08:40	Speech given by Li Wei, Director of Analysis & Testing Center of Baijin New Energy Company	Room 201
	08:40 – 09:10	Tea break & taking photos	Room 204
	09:10 – 11:50	"Introduction to New Products" presented by Dr. Martin	Room 201
	11:50 – 13:20	Lunch	Kaiyi Hall
	13:20 – 15:20	Expert report and interactive discussion	Room 201
	15:20 – 15:50	Tea break	Room 204
	15:50 – 17:30	Market analysis seminar	Room 201
	17:40	Dinner party	Tianxin Hall

Notes:
Theme: The 2nd Technical Seminar on New Energy Vehicles in China
Address: 990 Zhongshan Avenue, Xihu District, Hangzhou
Phone: 189××××5673
Contact: Candy
Email: Candy@****.com

 Task

J&K Publications is a publishing house located in Yichun. The company has invited James Peter, the writer of *A Brief History of Chinese Royal Gardens*, to attend the book launch. Professor Peter arrives in Yichun at 2 p.m. on July 24th and leaves at 10 a.m. on July 28th. During his stay, he will both work and go sightseeing. You are Lin Xi, a secretary at the reception department, and you are asked to make an itinerary for Professor Peter's trip.

Please make a reasonable itinerary for Professor James so that he can have an enjoyable stay in Yichun.

Date	Time	Event	Detail
July 24th	2 p.m.		
July 25th	8 a.m.		
	2 p.m.		
July 26th	8:30 a.m.		
	2:10 p.m.		
July 27th	9 a.m.		
	5 p.m.		
July 28th	7:30 p.m.		

Notes:

_____

_____

Ancient Chinese Wisdom

Read the following quote and answer the questions below.

Respect（敬）

Fan Chi asked the meaning of ren (benevolence). Confucius said, "Behave properly in your daily life, act with care and respect in dealing with others, and treat people with sincerity. You must not fail to do so even when you are in other countries. " (*The Analects*)

樊迟问仁。子曰："居处恭，执事敬，与人忠。虽之夷狄，不可弃也。"（《论语》）

(**Notes:** Benevolence is one of the core values of traditional Chinese culture and the highest moral standard for interpersonal interaction.)

1. Which one do you think is more important in the workplace, benevolence or benefits?

_____

2. How can we strike a balance benevolence and benefits in the workplace?

_____

Business Schedule	
Itinerary arrangements for Jack Ma and company executives Hangzhou to the United States June 2, 2012– June 6, 2012	
Date	**Schedule**
June 2nd, 2012 Saturday	7:00: Take a shuttle bus to Xiaoshan International Airport.
	7:55: Take flight CA1701 to Beijing (flight duration: approximately 2 hours and 5 minutes).
	10:00: Arrive at Beijing Capital International Airport and stay for 6 hours.
	16:00: Take flight CA985 to San Francisco Airport (flight duration: approximately 11 hours and 40 minutes).
	Arrive at San Francisco Airport at 3:40 Beijing time and 12:40 San Francisco time, and be picked up by Mr. Wang. Stay at the Hilton Hotel in San Francisco.
	18:00: Dine at Google cafeteria with company executives.
June 3rd, 2012 Sunday	Visit eBay. (accompanied by executives, gift in suitcase)
June 4th,2012 Monday	8:40: Take the bus to San Francisco Airport.
	10:05: Take flight AA6792 to Seattle (flight duration: 2 hours and 5 minutes).
	12:10: Learn how to make coffee by hand at Starbucks.
	20:34: Take flight B6176 to New York (flight duration: 7 hours and 21 minutes).
	3:55: Arrive at New York Airport, pick up by Mr. Zhang, and check in at the Pierre Hotel.
June 5th, 2012 Tuesday	8:50: Go to the headquarters to deliver a speech on the theme of "Embracing Entrepreneurship", calling for global entrepreneurs (the 01 document used is in the briefcase).
	16:50: Take CA982 first-class flight from Kennedy Airport in New York to Beijing (flight duration: approximately 13 hours and 30 minutes). The air tickets will be arranged in advance by Secretary Qin.
June 6th, 2012 Wednesday	18:20: Arrive at Capital International Airport at 18:20 on Wednesday, June 6, 2012, and take flight CA1710 to Xiaoshan International Airport at 19:00 (flight duration: 2 hours).
	21:00: Arrive at Xiaoshan International Airport at 21:00, pick up by Xiao Li from the company.
Notes: It will rain in the United States almost every day from June 1st to 18th, with only 3 days of normal temperature.	

Read the schedule above and decide whether the statements are true (T) or false (F).

(　　) 1. Jack Ma and the company executives will travel to the United kingdom for a business trip on June.

(　　) 2. They will take a direct flight from Hangzhou to San Francisco.

(　　) 3. They are going to visit eBay empty-handed.

(　　) 4. They will learn how to make coffee at Starbucks after arriving at Seattle.

(　　) 5. They will stay overnight in Seattle on June 4.

(　　) 6. Jack Ma is going to give an impromptu speech at 8:50 on June 5th.

(　　) 7. The weather in the United States will be rainy during their stay.

Unit 6 Receive a Business Client

Industry Outlook

To build a modern socialist country in all respects, we must, first and foremost, pursue high-quality development. Promoting green and low-carbon economic and social development is a key link in achieving high-quality development. Nature is the fundamental condition for human survival and development. Respecting, adapting to, and protecting nature is essential for building China into a modern socialist country in all respects. We must uphold and act on the principle that lucid waters and lush mountains are invaluable assets, and we must remember to maintain harmony between humanity and nature when planning our development.

The new energy industry is an important component of low-carbon development, among which the new energy vehicle industry holds a significant proportion. The development of new energy vehicles will become an important driving force for energy transformation. With the popularization of new energy vehicles, the consumption of traditional petroleum energy will gradually decrease, which will help reduce environmental pollution and carbon emissions, and promote the transformation and upgrading of energy structure.

The only direction for global automotive development is new energy, which has become a consensus among all countries and enterprises around the world. According to data from the China Association of Automobile Manufacturers, China's new energy vehicles are experiencing sustained explosive growth. As of the year 2023, China's new energy vehicle sales had been ranked first in the world for eight consecutive years.

New Concept Technology Co., Ltd. is a new energy vehicle company headquartered in Yichun. It has frequent and deep communication with a lot of new energy vehicle companies around the globe. A business partner is going to visit the company in a few days, and Jenny, the assistant manager at the marketing department, has been asked to receive the business partner at the airport.

● **Business Task**

Receiving a business client is quite important in business communications. Normally, the host company should get to know the basic information of the client first, such as his or her hobbies, arrival time, preferred accommodation and so on. During the client's stay, the host company should respect his or her custom and habit, and always be punctual when picking him or her up to events. When it is time to leave, the host company can bring some gifts to the client as a souvenir. A good reception will leave a good impression to the client and promote the business relations between the two parties; thus, create a win-win situation.

Words, Phrases and Sentences

Words and phrases concerning receiving a business client.

1. Translate the following words and phrases into Chinese or English.

○ **Develop**

develop a product _____

develop photos _____

develop relationship _____

发展生意 _____

冲洗照片 _____

形成习惯 _____

○ **Receive**

receive a business partner _____

receive a gift _____

receive signals _____

收到指令 _____

接待客人 _____

受到指责 _____

○ **Found**

found a company _____

be founded on respect   _____

well founded   _____

成立一家足球俱乐部   _____

基于互相信任   _____

创建一家投资机构   _____

2. Translate the following phrases into Chinese.

(1) receive an important business partner   _____

(2) arrange an appointment   _____

(3) financial difficulties   _____

(4) a tight schedule   _____

(5) a welcome banquet   _____

(6) a securities company   _____

(7) develop business ties   _____

(8) confirm the client's identity   _____

(9) leave a good impression to someone   _____

(10) make a small talk   _____

3. Translate the following phrases into English.

(1) 副总裁   _____

(2) 金融产品   _____

(3) 帮助他   _____

(4) 财政部门   _____

(5) 安排一辆车   _____

(6) 给你提供帮助   _____

(7) 持有一半股份   _____

(8) 误会某人   _____

(9) 一整年   _____

(10) 待得开心   _____

4. Find the words or phrases in the text with the meanings below and write them on the lines.

(1) _____ to think of or produce a new idea, product, etc. and make it successful

(2) _____ used especially in negative sentences and questions to emphasize that you do not like sb./sth.

(3) _____ sincere about sth.; not joking or meant as a joke

(4) _____ to say that you will not do sth. that sb. has asked you to do

(5) _____ having the usual qualities or features of a particular type of person, thing or group

(6) _____ good at learning, understanding and thinking in a logical way about things; showing this ability

(7) _____ the act of communicating with sb., especially regularly

(8) _____ any of the units of equal value into which a company is divided and sold to raise money

(9) _____ having or needing a lot of energy and enthusiasm

(10) _____ the act or process of getting ready for sth. or making sth ready

5. Complete the following sentences by filling in each blank with an appropriate word or phrase from the box below. Change its form if necessary.

typical	refuse	serious	stand	develop	intelligent

(1) Jenny is a very bright and _____ woman who knows clearly what she wants.

(2) Peter has politely _____ their invitation to the party.

(3) Giving money in a red envelope is a _____ Chinese custom when people go to weddings.

(4) Mr. White is a strict and _____ person who hardly smiles in front of the employees.

(5) The company has been _____ a new medicine and is likely to release it on the market in half a year.

(6) Your parents blame you simply because they can't _____ your bad habits!

(7) The child is _____ normally.

(8) The patient has the right to _____ treatment.

(9) This meal is _____ of local cookery.

(10) It is time to give _____ consideration to your choice.

6. Fill in the blanks with appropriate words.

(1) Tom is a responsible manager and always _____（参与）the daily management of the company.

(2) He is a hard-working and easy-going leader! You _____（错怪）him!

(3) Sanya attracts tourists from all over China because it has a mild weather _____ _____（全年）.

(4) If you have some friends to visit and don't know where to take them, the hot spring in Wentang Town _____（将会是个好的选择）.

(5) A very important partner is coming for a visit next week, and you are responsible to ____ _____（安排会面）with the CEO on Tuesday afternoon.

(6) When you meet your client for the first time, it is a good choice to _____ _____（开始交际）with weather.

7. Translate the following sentences into English.

(1) 现在我们将带您去酒店休息一下。

_____

(2) 我们真心希望 Mr. Brian 在北京待得愉快。

_____

(3) 明天我们将参加两个会议以及与市长座谈。

_____

(4) 总的来说广州一年四季的气候是比较温和的。

_____

(5) 谈到本地小吃，他可是非常在行的。

_____

Reading

I

Business reception is important, and the level of reception can reflect the overall image of a company. When it comes to conducting business receptions, attention should be paid to details to leave a good impression on guests.

To receive guests from foreign countries or local areas, the first step is to determine the name, composition, and total number of personnel to be received, confirm the train number and flight of the other party's arrival, and arrange for personnel who are equivalent to the guests' identities and positions to go to pick them up. To receive special VIPs, it is also necessary to prepare banners or posters, and give flowers as gifts when meeting. When going to the station or airport to meet guests, you should arrive early to prevent unexpected situations. Transportation should be prepared in advance. Do not wait until the guests arrive to hastily prepare transportation, as it will make the guests wait for a long time and delay the schedule. The etiquette of westerners when meeting for the first time is to embrace and kiss the cheek. However, easterners, especially Japanese people, are always polite and sometimes give a gift when meeting for the first time. Therefore, it is best to prepare a handbag in advance to avoid embarrassment.

After receiving the guests, you should first confirm their identity, and then introduce yourself to them. After a brief conversation at the airport, guide the guests to board the car and head for the hotel. On the way to the hotel, you can ask them about their feelings about the entire journey and their initial impression on the city, and introduce the city's characteristics, climate, cultural environment to them. At the same time, you can chat with the guests about their future work and travel plans in this city, and ask if they are satisfied with the arrangements and if they need to modify their itinerary. Be careful not to communicate with guests about itinerary arrangements as soon as they get on the car. Starting to discuss work without warming up can make the reception atmosphere slightly oppressive and dull. Sightseeing can be arranged in order to balance work and rest. If the tour activities are arranged properly, they will bring benefits to both sides in terms of business relations.

After arriving at the hotel, assist the guests in checking in and explain that you will come over the next morning to pick them up at the company, and then you can leave.

II

1. (At the airport.)

A: Excuse me, but are you Mr. Blake from Los Angeles?

B: Yes, I am.

A: I am from B&G Company. I am here to pick you up, and my name is Li Lei.

B: How do you do, Mr. Li? I'm glad to meet you!

A: Glad to meet you, too. Welcome to Guangzhou!

B: Thank you! It's very nice of you to come and meet me.

A: You are welcome. Oh, let me help you with your baggage.

B: Thanks a lot!

A: How was your flight?

B: On the whole, it's not bad except for a little turbulence.

A: How long was the trip?

B: 15 hours non-stop.

A: I think you must be exhausted. Hope you have a good rest after such a long trip!

B: Thank you!

A: Is this your first time in China?

B: No, I have visited China several times, but it's my first visit to Guangzhou and I think it's a great honor to be invited to this beautiful city.

A: It's our pleasure to have you here. I hope you will have a pleasant stay here.

B: Thank you very much. I'm sure I will have a wonderful time here.

2. (At the airport.)

A: Excuse me, are you Mr. Smith from the International Trading Corporation?

B: Yes.

A: I'm Andy, marketing assistant of B&G company. It is a pleasure to meet you.

B: Pleased to meet you.

A: Nice to meet you too. Welcome to Guangzhou. We have been expecting you ever since we received your email informing us of your arrival.

B: Thank you. We are very glad to meet you in Shanghai, and we hope that meeting in person will increase mutual understanding and boost business relations between us.

A: That's also our wishes. Our car is waiting over there. Please come with me, and we will take you to the Hotel in Pudong.

3. (In the car.)

A: Did you have a nice trip?

B: Well, it was kind of a long and tiring trip.

A: We have booked you a room in the hotel. It is a quiet and beautiful place, and you can have a good rest tonight.

B: Thank you very much. You are so considerate.

A: We have arranged a banquet in honor of your delegation at 6:30 p.m. tonight. The directors from our company board will all be present. I'll help you check in at the hotel, and you can have a rest for the afternoon. I will come to pick you up at the hotel one hour in advance.

B: That's very kind of you. I feel great honored.

Task

Suppose you are Jenny, an assistant manager at the marketing department of New Era Lithium Technology Co., Ltd.. You have just received Mr. White, a very important business partner from B&G company. You are going to take him to the hotel next and help him check in. In the car, you need to introduce a little about the city and brief him on the work schedule he is going to have during his stay in Yichun.

Now you are in the car with Mr. White, please write down the conversation.

Jenny: (1) _____ ?

Mr. White: It's a busy and modern city, and the people here are hospitable.

Jenny: Well, yes. people here in Guangzhou are quite nice. (2) _____ ?

Mr. White: Yes, it's much warmer here than where I come from, and I like this kind of weather.

Jenny: Glad you like it. (3) _____ ?

Mr. White: Well, it was quite a long flight! I couldn't sleep well all night!

Jenny: OK, then you must be exhausted. (4) _____ , and you can have a good rest there.

Mr. White: Great, thanks!

Jenny: I will take you to visit our company tomorrow morning, and then (5) _____ _____ . The CEO will join you for dinner at noon, and after that he will take you to experience traditional Chinese foot massage. That is your schedule for tomorrow.

Mr. White: OK, thanks for this considerate schedule!

Ancient Chinese Wisdom

Read the following quote and answer the questions below.

Rites（礼）

Rites are the basis for determining proper human relations, clarifying ambiguities, differentiating between things, and telling right from wrong. (*The Book of Rites*)

夫礼者所以定亲疏，决嫌疑，别同异，明是非也。(《礼记》)

(**Notes:** Rites are indispensable parts of workplace reception, showcasing the host's enthusiasm and sincerity. They also have impact on the business relationship between both parties.)

1. How important do you think rites are in business receptions?

_____

2. What are the polite ways to receive business clients?

_____

Extended Reading

Tips on how to receive a business client

1. Check with the client about his visit time, the list of personnel, positions, phone numbers, and other information to arrange corresponding receptions.

2. Discuss the visit itinerary with the client and communicate with the company. Once everything is finalized, send an email to the client for confirmation, while also preparing the company for reception.

3. Arrange hotels. Confirm if the client needs a hotel provided by the company. If yes, check details such as hotel star rating, location, room type, and facilities with the client. If no, provide assistance for his/her own booking.

4. Prepare meals and topics based on the client's nationality and religious beliefs.

5. Take the client to the hotel after picking up at the airport. Submit the visit itinerary and company information to the client, and finalize the visit schedule for the next day.

6. Pick up the client at the hotel on time the next day. Clients from different countries may have different perceptions of time, and Chinese companies generally wait for them in the hotel lobby 10 minutes in advance.

7. Meet with the client at the company. Conduct visits and meetings according to the itinerary, and arrange for a dedicated person to record the meeting content. Also arrange a multimedia conference room so that both parties can use projection slides to introduce their respective businesses.

8. Prepare a small gift to the client after the visit, usually with Chinese characteristics, such as tea, handicrafts, etc., and arrange entertainment activities such as sightseeing or shopping according to the client's demands.

9. Take the client to the airport after the visit is over. Before the plane takes off, call the customer to say goodbye.

10. Send the consensus, meeting minutes or memorandums through email to the client to urge the execution of the project.

Read the passage above and decide whether the statements are true (T) or false (F).

(　　) 1. The host should check with the client about detailed information including his/her marriage status.

(　　) 2. The host should always book a hotel for the client in advance because it is a good manner.

(　　) 3. The food and topics prepared should be based on the client's nationality and religious belief.

(　　) 4. The host can be 10 minutes late to pick up the client at the hotel the next day.

(　　) 5. It is usually a good manner to give some small gifts to the clients after he/she finishes the visit.

(　　) 6. The host should not contact with the client again after he/she goes back, because it may disturb him/her.

Unit 7 Write a Market Research Report

Scenario

Industry Outlook

We must adhere to the theme of promoting high-quality development and build a high-level socialist market economic system. Optimize the development environment of private enterprises, protect the property rights of private enterprises and the rights and interests of entrepreneurs in accordance with the law, and promote the development and growth of the private economy. Private economy plays a crucial role in the national economy. As an important part of China's national economy, private economy is an important driving force for economic growth and an important subject for promoting innovation. At the moment when the economy goes back on the normal track, it will also become an indispensable force for promoting high-quality economic development.

With the deepening of reform and opening-up, the private economy has gradually become the main engine of China's economic growth. As of the end of 2019, private enterprises accounted for over 90% of registered enterprises nationwide, accounting for over 60% of GDP and providing over 70% of employment opportunities.

According to statistics, private technology enterprises in China account for about 50% of the total number of high-tech enterprises in the country. About 65% of invention patents, 70% of technological innovation, and more than 80% of new products in the country come from private enterprises. In fields such as intelligent manufacturing, big data, logistics and warehousing, and biological health, private enterprises have firmly occupied a leading position. New economic and new business forms such as e-commerce, mobile payment, and shared bicycles have all been pioneered by private enterprises. In the past decade, the total number of private individuals employed in China has increased by over 200 million, contributing to over 80% of the employment. The annual average tax revenue growth of private enterprises is 8.3%, accounting for 59.6% of the national tax revenue. It has become a stabilizer for stable employment and an important contributor to tax revenue in China.

Green Papa is a chain baking company specializing in making healthy bread. Recently, the company has launched a new type of healthy bread that can fill the stomach while avoiding excessive fat and sugar intake. In order to promote this new product, Andy, the marketing assistant of the company, is required to conduct a market research and write a market research report, which is then reported to the marketing manager to help the company develop a promotion strategy for this new product.

● **Business Task**

A market research report, which decides the sales, market share and profit of a product, is decisive to a company. Before putting a new product into the market, a company should conduct a market research first to know the customers' acceptance. After the data is collected, the company should analyse it, and then writes a market research report based on the analysis, which should include basic facts of the product and future marketing strategies. A scientific market research report can help a company boost sales of a certain product, and also helps to improve the company's profit and competitiveness.

Words, Phrases and Sentences

Words and phrases concerning writing a market research report.

1. Translate the following words and phrases into Chinese or English.

○ **Market**

farmer's market _____

local market _____

on the market _____

全球市场 _____

市场规模 _____

市场份额 _____

○ **Research**

market research _____

a research project _____

research into
研究论文 _____
展开研究 _____
医学研究 _____

○ **Interview**

interview a consumer _____

street interview _____

call for an interview _____

随机采访 _____

会见某人 _____

独家采访 _____

2. Translate the following phrases into Chinese.

(1) development trend _____

(2) account for _____

(3) fat free _____

(4) come to a conclusion _____

(5) conduct a market research _____

(6) on the increase _____

(7) domestic market _____

(8) promote sales _____

(9) job market _____

(10) job interview _____

3. Translate the phrases into English.

(1) 每周例会 _____

(2) 市场调研 _____

(3) 最新产品 _____

(4) 功能型饮料 _____

(5) 提供优惠券 _____

(6) 自动售卖机 _____

(7) 蓝领 _____

(8) 向某人汇报 _____

(9) 解决 _____

(10) 开展更多促销 _____

4. Find the words in the text with the meanings below and write them on the lines.

(1) _____ a small shop which sells mainly food and which is usually open until late at night

(2) _____ to help sth. to happen or develop

(3) _____ to announce sth. on a newspaper, on television, or on a bulletin board

(4) _____ a flat raised structure, usually made of wood, that people stand on when they make speeches or give a performance

(5) _____ people who work in offices rather than doing physical work such as making things in factories or building things

(6) _____ the container or covering that sth. is sold in

(7) _____ a machine from which you can get things such as cigarettes, chocolate, or coffee by putting in money and pressing a button

(8) _____ a reduction in the usual price of sth.

(9) _____ a piece of printed paper which allows you to pay less money than usual for a product, or to get it free

(10) _____ work that involves studying sth. and trying to discover facts about it

5. Complete the following sentences by filling in each blank with an appropriate word from the box below. Change its form if necessary.

| interview   frequency   channel   effectively   present   feature |

(1) Can you come now? I know it's _____ , but I have something urgent to discuss.

(2) Betty has already _____ the prizes to the winners.

(3) The police _____ the driver, but had no evidence to go on.

(4) The _____ of John's phone calls increased rapidly.

(5) She spent two years in _____ this topic.

(6) The government will surely use diplomatic _____ to solve this problem.

(7) Nowadays it's very popular to buy drinks from _____ in office buildings.

(8) People can always get a good _____ on Black Friday.

(9) With a _____ , you can save some money when you buy this air conditioner.

(10) He has carried out extensive _____ into new energy vehicles.

6. Fill in the blanks with appropriate words.

(1) I'm _____ （制订计划） to help you lose 10 pounds this summer.

(2) The supervisor has asked him to _____ （写一份报告） about how to increase sales.

(3) It is reported that about 90% of the people _____ （上网） every day.

(4) He is a sports lover and he often _____ （健身） in the gym.

(5) Can you offer _____ （详细的信息） about the energy drink market in

Macao?

7. Translate the following sentences into English.

(1) 我昨天尝了你们的新饮料，味道非常好。

_____

(2) 老实说，我比较喜欢在便利店买饮料。

_____

(3) 请你写一份市场调研报告并于本周五前交给经理。

_____

(4) 你们应该通过多种渠道给你们的新产品打广告。

_____

(5) 能量型饮料对我没有太大吸引力。

_____

Reading

I

Market research is the use of scientific methods to purposefully and systematically collect, organize, and analyze various intelligence, information, and materials related to supply, demand, and resources. It grasps the current supply and demand situation and development trends, providing correct basis for enterprises to make marketing strategies and decisions.

Market research reports are based on the investigation and understanding of the actual situation of a product. They analyze and study all the information and materials obtained through the investigation, reveal the essence, find patterns, summarize experiences, and finally present them in written form, which is the research report.

The components of a market research report are title, date, personnel, location, method and the main body. The main body is the core of the market research report, and the data cited in the main body should be true and valid. It should explain the investigation completely and accurately, analyze the data scientifically, and then give suggestions reasonably. The following aspects should be included in the main body of a market research report.

1. Introduction. Investigators should give an introduction to the basic information obtained through the survey, which is the foundation of the entire text. They should clearly describe the historical and current situations of the product, including market share, consumption, output and price.

2. Analysis and prediction. They refer to the prediction of market development trends based

on the analysis of the information obtained from the survey, and they directly affect the decision-making of relevant enterprise leaders. The method of discussion should be used to analyze the data one by one, conduct scientific research, and form conclusive opinions.

3. Marketing suggestions. This part reflects the purpose of writing a market research report. Based on the previous investigations and analyses, specific suggestions and measures should be proposed for decision-makers to refer to. Pay attention to the pertinence and feasibility of the suggestions, so that they really contribute to solving problems.

A qualified market research report should have a very clear framework, and a concise and clear data analysis results. Typical market research reports have a fixed pattern, and we should adjust the form and style of the report according to different needs of different projects, so that the market research reports can have a richer connotation.

II

This survey is conducted in order to gain a deeper understanding of the consumption situation of households in the alcohol and catering markets in × city. The survey was conducted by ×× University from July to August 2022, using a questionnaire-based interview survey. The total number of samples selected for this survey was 2,000 households. After the completion of various investigation work, the university has summarized the investigation content, and its market research report is as follows.

1. Consumption of alcoholic products

White spirit is consumed more than red wine. The reasons are as follows: first, white spirit is mainly used for gifts, while red wine is mainly used for self consumption; second, most of the advertisements of businesses are for white spirit, and few are for red wine. As a result, the market of white spirit is larger than that of red wine.

In terms of white spirit consumption, customer loyalty survey shows that consumers who frequently change brands account for 32.95% of the total sample, and those who occasionally change brands take up 43.75%. Those who like new brands of liquor occupy 32.39% of the total sample, those who do not care 52.27% and those who explicitly express their dislike 3.4%.

2. Consumption of dietary products

This survey mainly focuses on some restaurants and the foods that consumers prefer. The consumption has the following important characteristics.

(1) Consumers mostly choose to consume in places around their work places or residences, with a certain regional significance.

(2) Consumers pursue fashion consumption. For example, consumers consume more lobsters, sweet and sour ribs, and Kung Pao Chicken, especially lobsters, which account for 26.14% of the total survey sample, and occupy the catering market with absolute advantage.

(3) Every time they dine with friends, the average consumption amount per consumer is around 50 yuan.

3. Conclusion

(1) The consumption level of residents in this city is not too high, and their income is on an average level.

(2) In terms of consumption of alcoholic products, residents mainly use white spirit for their own consumption, while the consumption of red wine is relatively small. The brands of alcoholic products used for personal consumption, whether white spirit or red wine, are mainly domestic brands.

(3) Consumers pay more attention to the price, quality, packaging, and promotion of alcohol when buying alcoholic products, and a considerable number of consumers hold an indifferent attitude.

Task

New Era Lithium Technology Co., Ltd. has developed a new energy car, and plans to put it on the market next year. In order to know people's intention of buying this new type of car and make marketing strategies, it has conducted a market research. The market research results are as follows.

Percentage of Potential Customers	Factors that Influence People's Intention of Purchase
32%	the price of the car
19%	the appearance of the car
49%	the function of the car

Please write a market research report according to the information above.

A Market Research Report on the Newly-developed New Energy Car	
Introduction	
Aim	
Results	
Conclusions	

Ancient Chinese Wisdom

Read the following quote and answer the questions below.
Being Sincere in Thought（诚意）

Being sincere in thought is of primary importance in self-cultivation. (*Annotations on The Great Learning* by Zhu Xi)

诚其意者，自修之首也。（朱熹《大学章句》）

(**Notes:** Sincerity is the fundamental principle of being a person and an important foundation of a company, which is related to its long-term development and gaining consumer trust.)

1. Do you think a company should be sincere to its customers? Why?

_____

2. What consequences will be there if a company deceives its customers?

_____

Extended Reading

Market Research Report on "Happy Sleep" Therapy

1. Market overview

One third of the people around the world have sleep problems. A survey by the American Sleep Foundation shows that there are 84 diseases related to sleep. Adults who sleep less than 6.5 hours can develop a "sleep deficit" and "health overdraft", shortening their lifespan. Long term insomnia can reduce the body's immune function. Youth insomnia can affect the secretion of growth hormone in the body, thereby affecting growth and development, intellectual development, and endocrine regulation. Long term insomnia in young and middle-aged women can speed up the aging of their appearance.

2. Market demand

People need revolutionary solutions with clear therapeutic effects and without significant side effects. But currently, sleep therapy products are mainly based on drugs, which can easily become addictive after long-term use. And health supplements are not easily recognized by insomnia patients either due to their uncertain efficacy. In addition, medical institutions lack a professional treatment team, resulting in unsatisfactory therapeutic effects. The sleep market urgently needs a professional team to provide personalized, safe, reliable, dependency free, and side effect free "green therapies"

3. Feasibility of "Happy Sleep" Therapy

The "Happy Sleep" therapy has opened up the best solution for improving human sleep to date. It integrates bio-electronics, traditional Chinese medicine economics, diet, and other sciences, adopting personalized and customized principles to form a unique "Happy Sleep" management system, elevating the traditional single method to a sleep management system. The therapy, which has a good hypnotic effect on people with various sleep disorders, advocates for a healthy and green comprehensive treatment method with no side effects. This therapy will attract quite a lot of consumers as long as reasonable marketing strategies are adopted, as it is effective and meets market demand.

Read the passage above and decide whether the statements are true (T) or false (F).

(　　) 1. Lack of sleep may lead to the shortening of lifespan in adults.

(　　) 2. The word "insomnia" in line 4, paragraph 1 means good sleep.

(　　) 3. If a woman cannot sleep at night for a long term, her appearance will age faster.

(　　) 4. Drugs are good choices with no side effects to treat insomnia.

(　　) 5. The "Happy Sleep" therapy will win quite a lot of customers according to the author.

Unit 8 Introduce a New Product

Industry Outlook

The report of the 20th National Congress of the Communist Party of China proposed that we must regard innovation as our primary driver of growth. Innovation is an inexhaustible driving force for the development and progress of a country or a nation, and an important force in promoting the progress of human society.

Innovation is multifaceted, including theoretical innovation, institutional innovation, scientific and technological innovation, cultural innovation, etc. We need to strengthen the dominant position of enterprises in scientific and technological innovation, and better transform scientific and technological strength into industrial competitive advantages.

Therefore, we should actively improve innovation capabilities, enhance product added value, and transform scientific and technological strength into enterprise competitiveness. In the meantime, when we plan to promote new products, we should be familiar with product innovation technologies, product characteristics, etc., enhance product added value, and actively transform technological power into product competitiveness.

Business Task

Introducing a new product is a common business of companies. At the same time, product introductions are very important for companies as they can effectively convey the value of products, attract consumers, and ultimately promote sales. When introducing a product, it is important to be concise and focused on highlighting the value and benefits of the product. Use clear language and intuitive examples to help the target customers better understand and identify with the advantages of the product. At the same time, with different customer groups, adjust the tone and content style to better fit the needs and interests of the target customers.

Words, Phrases and Sentences

Words and phrases concerning new product.

1. Translate the following words and phrases into Chinese or English.

○ **Product**

present a new product　　　　_____

product introduction　　　　_____

sell product　　　　_____

推广产品　　　　_____

产品策略　　　　_____

产品定位　　　　_____

○ **Customer**

target customer　　　　_____

customer demand　　　　_____

regular customer　　　　_____

吸引客户　　　　_____

潜在客户　　　　_____

客户满意度　　　　_____

○ **Introduction**

product introduction　　　　_____

introduce a new design　　　　_____

introduce a new concept　　　　_____

介绍演讲　　　　_____

筹备产品介绍　　　　_____

引进外资　　　　_____

2. Translate the following phrases into Chinese.

(1) product characteristics　　　　_____

(2) advantage　　　　_____

(3) target customer   _____

(4) price strategy   _____

(5) market research   _____

(6) customer concern   _____

(7) launch a product   _____

(8) product catalogue   _____

(9) after-sales service   _____

(10) selling point   _____

(11) customers' requirements   _____

(12) special offer   _____

(13) product introduction   _____

(14) product's feature   _____

(15) satisfy customers' needs   _____

3. Translate the following phrases into English.

(1) 旅行套餐   _____

(2) 旅行社   _____

(3) 满足某人的需求   _____

(4) 目的地   _____

(5) 集体旅行   _____

(6) 关注某人的需求   _____

(7) 负担花销   _____

(8) 人事经理   _____

(9) 旅游景点   _____

(10) 相对较低   _____

4. Find the words or phrases in the text with the meanings below and write them on the lines.

(1) _____ the money that you pay to travel by plane

(2) _____ the act of telling sb. that sth. is good or useful or that sb. would be suitable for a particular job, etc.

(3) _____ a feeling of worry, especially one that is shared by many people

(4) _____ a feature of sth. that makes people want to buy or use it

(5) _____ a type of accommodation in a hotel, etc. that includes all meals

(6) _____ a person or thing that is not included in sth.

(7) _____ a journey to a place and back again

(8) _____ to make sth. available for use for the first time

(9) _____ to think that sth. will happen

(10) _____ to decide how sth. will be made

5. Complete the following sentences by filling in each blank with an appropriate word or phrase from the box below. Change its form if necessary.

airfare	full board	round-trip	relatively	selling point
tourist site	concern	exclusion	airport transfer	check-in

(1) The _____ fare to Shanghai is CNY 800 yuan.

(2) Our main _____ is to provide quality travel package which is perfect to customers.

(3) Mingyue Mountain is one of the most popular _____ in Jiangxi.

(4) What's the _____ from Nanchang to Changchun?

(5) Madam, if you need to transfer, please report to the _____ desk.

(6) This travel package provides _____ so we don't need to worry about the meals.

(7) Before you sign a contract, you need to check the list of _____ in the contract.

(8) The _____ of this product is its conveniency.

(9) All the passengers must _____ at least one and a half hours before departure time.

(10) _____ speaking, this travel agency provides good travel packages.

6. Fill in the blanks with appropriate words.

(1) This travel package gives a 10% _____ （折扣）to parties of more than 50.

(2) We need to _____ （考虑）how to meet customers' needs.

(3) Please do not _____ （顾虑）to contact our Customer Service Department.

(4) Are you still _____ （寻找）a resort for your winter holiday?

(5) Our company aims to _____ （提供）assistance to people in need.

7. Translate the following sentences into English.

(1) 我们的产品能够完美解决您的问题。

_____

(2) 我们的旅行套餐能为您提供一段满意且难忘的经历。

_____

(3) 人数超过 20 人的游客团体享受八折。

_____

(4) 同时，我们还提供全食宿服务。

_____

(5) 假如您对我们的套餐感兴趣，尽请与我们联系。

Reading

I
How to Introduce a New Product

Wonder if you are a salesperson who just enters the market, and just in time you have in your hands a winning product—one that's going to win you many loyal customers, and take your business to the next level.

The future in front of you is just wonderful except for one thing. You aren't sure how to introduce your remarkable product to your customers. And until you figure this out, the customers have already gone with the experienced sales managers. That would definitely be a nightmare.

So, if you don't want things to be like that, and if you want your business to be successful, it is particularly important to prepare a perfect plan for the new product introduction. Besides, to let your customers know the product that you want to sell, or even to make them to be eager to buy your product, giving them a product introduction is one of the best ways to do. But how to introduce a new product? Here are four steps that you can follow to make your own product introduction.

Step 1: Start with a question.

Always start with a question. Ask your customers a question which concerns them the most. Of course, the question must come from extensive market research and must be based on reliable supporting data. Or maybe, just ask them the most simple question like, "Are you still looking for...? "

Step 2: Show your solutions.

As long as you know the customers' needs, it would be the time you show them your solutions. Always show them the positive points of your product. You must make them have motivates and desires to buy your product. After carefully understanding your customers, you position your wonderful product into their world. It can go like, "with a well-organised..., a high-quality..., and a decent price, our product will provide you a.... "

Step 3: Focus on the benefits.

You must be clear that customers have plenty options. One of the most important things to them is how much benefits they can get from buying your product. You must persuade them to buy yours but not others' by showing how much more benefits they can get from yours than from others' products. Those will make your product more competitive. Remember to describe as more details as possible to make sure the customers know what benefits they can get if they buy.

Step 4: Call to action.

Now comes the last step. You have introduced all the details and benefits of your product, and the last thing you need to do is to make your customers move. Try to offer them a 10% or 15% discount to attract them to buy your product, but don't offer too much discount in case you lose your money in business.

II
Tips for writing a product introduction

When you are selling a product, either online or offline, one of the key things that you need to do is writing the product introduction. If you're writing a product introduction, take some time to think before you start to do it. Research your product and the target customers so you know how to best sell the product. Remember, always start with a great opening and then describe the product vividly in a couple of short sentences. These are some tips that you can follow before writing a product introduction.

1. Target your customers.

Who are you targeting with this product? That's a vital question to ask. Common characteristics to consider when trying to determine the target customers include age, gender, income level, buying habits, occupation, family status,location,education level, hobbies and interests.

For example, when you're selling hot spring travel packages for a local company.Try to connect your hot spring travel packages to the target customer's objective and travel habits. Companies will prefer to a trip that can build team spirit or that can comfort business customers in an affordable budget. Family-oriented people will respond to descriptions of comfort journey and tasty food of hot spring hotels.

2. Connect the product's features to its benefits.

Consumers generally buy products that provide them specific benefits. Before writing a product introduction, ask yourself, "What would a customer gain from my product?"

Make a list of the features or characteristics of your product. From there, try to link these to a benefit for customers. This will help you get a sense of what to focus on as you write your introduction.For the hot spring travel packages example, try connecting the travel comfort, tasty food, beautiful scenery, or the decent price of the travel package to its benefits.

3. Make a list of descriptive words.

Impressive introduction can really make your product sound attractive to potential customers. To start introduction, make a list of words that remind you of your product and find ways to make these words pop.

When you describe a journey, the first word that may come to mind may be things like comfort, happy, and unforgettable. Are there any ways you can make those words to sound more special? Instead of using terms like "comfort" and "happy," you could find something more special or unique. For example, you could say the hot spring travel package "bring you a feeling like warm spring."

4. Start with a great opening.

When writing a product introduction, you have limited time to get a consumer's attention. Use that time wisely. Asking a question that grabs the reader's attention can help you win at the first step.

In the hot spring travel packages example, you can ask your audiences to imagine. For example, say something like, "Are you looking for a travel that can bring you a warm and cozy memory in cold winter?"

5. Check carefully before presenting.

Always be careful with anything you write before presenting it to your customers. Before submitting your product introduction, you need to proofread again and again until you can be sure that it is perfect.

||| Task

Suppose you are Lily Smith, a trip adviser from Mingyue Mountain Happy Life Group, a travel agency in Mingyue Mountain tourist site. S&G Ltd.,a Thai company wants to organize a group trip for its staff. John Wallace, the secretary of administrative department from S&G Ltd. has found your company for recommendation. Now you are going to introduce your new travel package to John and other staff.

4D3N Love me, take me to Mingyue Mountain For only 20,000 yuan/person	
Itinerary	Day 1: Bangkok-Kunming-Yichun 　　　　Arrival, meet and transfer to hotel, hotel check-in Day 2: Mingyue Mountain 　　· Moon Bay Culture Garden 　　· Yungu Bathing in Moonlight Statue 　　· Zhu Xi Poem Pavilion 　　· The Xingyue Cave & Trestle over Blue Sky Day 3: Wentang Town 　　· Gujingquan Street 　　· Nanre Village 　　· Mingyue Romance Park 　　· Yangshan Qiyin Temple 　　· Tianmu Hot Spring Day 4: Yichun-Kunming-Bangkok 　　　　Departure flight to Bangkok

Travel Date	March 3rd–6th; March 21st–24th; April 10–13th; April 23rd–26th; May 5–8th
Flight Schedule	Bangkok-Kunming-Yichun (BKK-KMG-YIC) Flight No.8L802; Flghit No.8L9887 6:05 p.m. – (the next day) 9:45 a.m. Yichun-Kunming-Bangkok (YIC-KMG-BKK) Flight No.8L9888; Flight No.8L801 4:10 p.m. – (the next day) 5:05 p.m.
Inclusions	· Round-trip airfare (Bangkok-Yichun-Bangkok) · Free 10kg hand-carried baggage and 20kg check-in baggage · 3 days/2 nights hotel accommodation at Tianmu Hot Spring Hotel · Full board meals (breakfast, lunch and dinner as per itinerary) · Round-trip airport transfers (airport-hotel-airport) · Bankok terminal fee · China group visa processing · Travel insurance
Exclusions	· Tickets to the tourist sites

Now complete the travel package introduction according to the information provided.

4D3N Love me, take me to the Mingyue Mountain

Are you still looking for a wonderful and fascinating trip for your staff ? Have you ever wondered about ancient Zen culture? Do you want to experience an excellent hot spring trip? With a well-ordered itinerary, superior services and a decent price, our travel package from Bangkok to Yichun will provide your staff with an unique experience worth recalling!

_____

_____

_____

_____

_____

_____

_____

If you are interested in this travel package, please don't hesitate to contact us. We are offering a 20% discount for groups of more than 20 people. We can also provide other personalized customization service to satisfy different customers' needs. I believe we can provide you with an extraordinary experience!

Ancient Chinese Wisdom

Read the following quote and answer the questions below.

Talk Substance; Act with Perseverance（言有物，行有恒）

A man of virtue should talk substance and act with perseverance. (*The Book of Changes*)

君子以言有物而行有恒。（《周易》）

(**Notes:** What one talks or writes about should have a sound basis and substance; the language and words he uses should fit the actual context. Hyperbole, exaggeration or falsehood should be opposed. In doing anything, one must have perseverance and focus, stick to principle and honor his words. One should preserve until the goal is met and must never give up halfway. This term also means that one should take a realist approach, seek truth and act in good faith.)

1. What truths are revealed from the above quote?

_____

2. How would you talk substance and act with perseverance in your daily life?

_____

Extended Reading

SLZ club introduction

This is a gathering place for vinyl enthusiasts. Friends who like or are interested in vinyl can visit us! If you want to ask what activities are in our club, I believe that the following introduction will not disappoint you.

Monthly themed recording experience meeting

SLZ CLUB members have the opportunity to decide the theme of each event every month, and each time they participate in the experience will require participants to wear clothes that match the theme. At the experience meeting, participants can carry out various activities and experience the scene created by the theme album in an immersive experience.

Private Record Appreciation Hall

SLZ CLUB will provide you with a relatively private venue to share and exchange your favorite records with like-minded friends, and the staff will also provide you with other services.

Music dining bar

We will provide you with different types of meals at different time periods. You can come to the restaurant to dine at any time, and we will continue to play records for you. If you have any special records you want to listen to, you can talk to the staff.

Record supermarket

SLZ CLUB will provide you with classic or current popular records here. You can listen to and buy them here, and the decoration here will not disappoint you. We will create an area with the theme, and you can find it here. Check in at the checkout, and drinks will be provided to everyone at the checkout.

Private custom recordings

Want to record a record of your own? SLZ CLUB will provide members with a recording studio to make a record of their own, and will also provide DIY materials for everyone. If you are interested in it, please come and experience it.

Record collection management

Still struggling with no place to collect records or no time to clean them? SLZ CLUB will provide you with collection management services, you can rest assured to keep yourself here, we will regularly arrange staff to clean and maintain it for you.

Record exhibitions

At the end of each year, the SLZ CLUB holds a exhibition. We will not only show you records, but we will also show you the general production process of vinyl records, and we will also set up small exhibition halls with special themes. At the same time, the photos and audios of the theme experience sessions mentioned above will also be available for everyone to do a retrospective.

Record maintenance and repair

Partners will no longer have to worry about finding a place to repair if there is damage on the record in the future. SLZ CLUB will provide you with maintenance and repair services for records, so there is no need to worry about the problem of damaged records.

SLZ CLUB is about to meet you, friends who are interested in vinyl records can come and visit! Looking forward to your arrival! Repost our Weibo and three people will be randomly selected to receive a mystery vinyl record!

(　　) 1. SLZ CLUB is a gathering place for people_____.

        A. who love pop music

        B. who love vinyl record

        C. who love classic record

        D. who love DIY food

(　　) 2. What does "immersive experience" mean?

        A. An experience that seeming to surround the audience, player, etc. so that they feel completely involved.

        B. An experience that people can feel as if they are in real three-dimensional space by images and sounds that are produced by a computer and connected equipment.

C. A show of the work an artist has done in their life so far.

D. An event at which objects such as paintings are shown to the public.

(   ) 3. What can you do in the SLZ CLUB?

A. Record a record of your own.

B. Share and exchange your favorite records with like-minded friends.

C. Listen to and buy classic or current popular records.

D. All of the above

(   ) 4. What service does SLZ CLUB offer to customer?

A. Holding small concert monthly.

B. Shooting movies for customers.

C. Providing customers with maintenance and repair services for records.

D. Providing DIY cellphone cases for customers.

(   ) 5. What can we know from this passage?

A. At SLZ CLUB, customers will no longer worry about collecting records or no time to clean them.

B. SLZ CLUB is an outdoor club.

C. Everyone who has reposted SLZ CLUB's Weibo can get a vinyl record.

D. SLZ CLUB only provide customers with maintenance services for records.

Unit 9 — Reply to Customer Queries

Scenario

Industry Outlook

The 133rd China Import and Export Fair (Canton Fair) came to a successful conclusion in Guangzhou on May 5th, 2023. It is the largest Canton Fair in history. The overall operation is stable, and the goal of "efficiency, security, digital, and green" has been achieved.

The report of the 20th National Congress of the Communist Party of China put forward the requirement of promoting the high-quality construction of the the Belt and Road, and the China Import and Export Fair also provided such an opportunity to make new customers, explore new opportunities, regain growth confidence, and promote the smooth trade in the construction of the the Belt and Road.

For China, the Canton Fair is a bridge for companies to go global. For the world, the Canton Fair creates opportunities for enterprises from various countries and regions to collaborate with Chinese enterprises to build a safe, reliable, and efficient supply chain.

The demand for overseas buyers at this year's Canton Fair is mainly in Southeast Asia, and in the past few years, the penetration rate of online e-commerce in countries such as Europe and America has sharply increased. Therefore, cross-border e-commerce exhibitions have become one of the highlights of this year's Canton Fair and a new form of international trade.

With cultural confidence and the rise of domestic products, domestic companies continue to increase technological investment and develop new products to meet overseas personalized needs. The global competitiveness of Chinese products is constantly improving.

Innovation has become a bright label of the Canton Fair. Exhibiting companies, products, and services are innovating with higher technological content. This year's exhibitors brought over 800,000 new products. Exhibitors have been accelerating the transformation and upgrading of traditional industries through innovative ideas, optimized designs and improved technology. With an innovative spirit, we Chinese strive for excellence. Made in China and created in China make every Canton Fair unique.

● **Business Task**

Companies from various industries are setting up booths at the fair. When we attend a fair to promote our products, we need to explain our products' features to potential customers. Replying to customer queries can make or break a business. Providing relevant information and using appropriate expressions are very important. We should be well-prepared before attending a fair.

To answer customers' queries about our products, we must learn specific information about the exhibited items, such as price, MOQ, delivery etc. It may be helpful to think about what questions customers are likely to ask about a product in a fair.

Words, Phrases and Sentences

Words and phrases concerning reply to customer queries.

1. Translate the following words and phrases into Chinese or English.

○ **Price**

market price _____

wholesale price _____

retail price _____

降价 _____

促销价 _____

税后价格 _____

○ **Brand**

brand leader _____

brand choice _____

brand loyalty _____

品牌形象 _____

全新的，崭新的 _____

品牌知名度　　　　　　　　　_____

○ **Delivery**

prompt delivery　　　　　　　_____

pay on delivery　　　　　　　_____

payment before delivery　　　_____

免费送货　　　　　　　　　　_____

交货日期　　　　　　　　　　_____

交货周期　　　　　　　　　　_____

2. Translate the following phrases into Chinese.

(1) packaging　　　　　　　　_____

(2) QR code　　　　　　　　　_____

(3) showcase　　　　　　　　　_____

(4) advertisement　　　　　　　_____

(5) brochure　　　　　　　　　_____

(6) customize　　　　　　　　　_____

(7) guarantee　　　　　　　　　_____

(8) franchise　　　　　　　　　_____

(9) after-sales service　　　　　_____

(10) AOV(average order value)　_____

3. Translate the following phrases into English.

(1) 工艺美术品公司　　　　　　_____

(2) 进出口交易会　　　　　　　_____

(3) 潜在客户　　　　　　　　　_____

(4) 商务会展　　　　　　　　　_____

(5) 产品目录　　　　　　　　　_____

(6) 交付周期　　　　　　　　　_____

(7) 最低起订量　　　　　　　　_____

(8) 离岸价格　　　　　　　　　_____

(9) 热销商品　　　　　　　　　_____

(10) 最终确认　　　　　　　　　_____

4. Find the words or phrases in the text with the meanings below and write them on the lines.

(1) _____ an event at which people, businesses, etc. show and sell their goods

(2) _____ to show sth. in a public place for people to enjoy or to give them information

(3) _____ a question, especially one asking for information or expressing a doubt about sth.

(4) _____ an amount of money that is taken off the usual cost of sth.

(5) _____ to be greater than a particular number or amount

(6) _____ bringing letters, parcels, or other goods to someone's house or to another place where they want them

(7) _____ the limits between which sth. varies

(8) _____ describe sth. that can develop into sth. or be developed in the future

(9) _____ a person that you work with, especially in a profession or a business

(10) _____ a judgement that you make without having the exact details or figures about the size, amount, cost, etc. of sth.

5. Complete the following sentences by filling in each blank with an appropriate word or phrase from the box below. Change its form if necessary.

exceed	negotiate	range	estimate	colleague
query	handle	catalogue	potential	immediate

(1) It is _____ that the project will last four years.

(2) There will be an increase in the _____ of 0 to 3 percent.

(3) The secretary makes her a little bit wait for a second, the meeting ought end _____ _____ .

(4) Please do not hesitate to contact me if you have any _____ .

(5) We need to be able to _____ pressure in this job.

(6) The production costs of our new products have _____ $100,000.

(7) The news of her promotion went over well with her _____ .

(8) The company is being actively considered as a _____ partner.

(9) There were reports that three companies were _____ to market the dishwasher.

(10) The _____ gives a full description of each product.

6. Fill in the blanks with appropriate words.

(1) There will be around 10 _____（投递）a week.

(2) The goods are to be _____（包装）in strong but small wooden cases.

(3) If the quantity exceeds 200 sets，we will _____（减价）our price by 10%.

(4) Please pay attention to avoid any possible _____（运途损坏）.

(5) _____（严格质量控制）ensures the higher quality of products.

7. Translate the following sentences into English.

(1) 该货物已做好立即交付的准备了。

_____

(2) 包装应由卖方选择。

_____

(3) 所有报价以我方最终确认为准。

_____

(4) 折扣取决于订单的大小。

_____

(5) 如果您订购 500 件以上，我们可以给予 30% 的折扣。

_____

Reading

I

Customer Service Skills

Today's customer service involves much more than face-to-face conversations or answering phone calls. With the proliferation of digital service channels and the growing demands of tech-savvy consumers, customer service roles have become more challenging.

Apart from good product knowledge, service agents need to have a full range of customer service/support skills to successfully perform their work duties. Thus, It's necessary to provide the level of service consumers expect.

Despite the wide adoption of artificial intelligence and self-service technologies, human-to-human interactions are still key to delivering an outstanding customer service experience. Today, 59% of all consumers feel companies have lost touch with the human element of customer experience. And when it comes to providing excellent service experience, it's the soft skills that create the difference between an average service agent and the one who can really delight and "wow" your customers.

What is a hard skill? To put it simply, a hard skill can be taught through training, school, or practice. Examples of hard skills can differ based on the industry. Here are some hard skill examples: language proficiency, management skills, typing speed, or a certificate/degree.Hard skills, like specialized knowledge or technical abilities, are important. However, soft skills are becoming more critical.In essence, soft skills in customer-facing positions are paramount.

Here are some of the most basic customer service skills that every employee, whose job includes interacting with customers, should master.

1. Effective listening

Active listening can be found on almost any customer service skill set list. Effective listening means being focused and fully present in the conversation. Therefore, you can truly understand what the person on the other end is trying to say. Good listening skills can help agents avoid misunderstandings, handle service issues faster, and be more efficient. Studies show that most people tend to remember only 25% to 50% of what they hear. Thus, developing good listening skills is essential for face-to-face and voice interactions.

2. Attentiveness

Attentiveness is one of the key skills in customer service. Being attentive to all the details the customer is sharing allows agents to target the problem precisely and avoid miscommunication. Since customers demand a personalized experience, service reps require a great level of attentiveness to make interactions more personal. Even when they have to stick to certain canned responses, attentiveness can ensure the dialogue remains meaningful and personalized for each customer.

3. Patience

Service agents have to deal with unhappy customers on a daily basis. Thus, patience is one of the most essential customer service soft skills you can have. Demonstrating self-control and the ability to stay calm in challenging service scenarios can help diffuse tense situations with frustrated customers. It also takes patience to professionally interact with customers who struggle to describe the problem or follow the agent's guidelines/instructions.

4. Empathy

Empathy is the ability to sense and share the emotions of others. It is a must-have customer service skill. Showing concern, caring, and understanding can go a long way, especially when interacting with complaining customers. Given that 70% of buying experiences are based on how the customers feel, they are being treated. It comes to show that empathy allows you to create emotional connections with customers which is the foundation of a good customer service experience.

5. Clear communication skills

Clear communication is one of the most important customer service skills for everyone working in customer-oriented positions. Both oral and written communication skills matter equally. Using unclear language, slang, specific jargon, mumbling, or being unable to get the message across in a clear and concise manner can create customer dissatisfaction. Communication skills are also interlinked with the ability to use positive language, which is discussed below.

6. Ability to use positive language

The ability to use positive language is among the most desired skills needed for customer service. How service agents phrase their responses can have a big impact on the way customers perceive your company. Saying "This product will be available next week", instead of "We don't have this product right now", makes it easier for customers to accept the information. Therefore, using a positive sentence structure can create a better impression of your customer service.

7. Problem-solving skills

Good customer service basically means getting to the core of the problem and immediately coming up with the right solution. With excellent problem-solving skills, agents can address challenging service issues more efficiently and make appropriate decisions, while also being able to think proactively and creatively if a problem arises. Moreover, problem-solving skills also help service agents manage conflicts and deal with unhappy customers.

8. Positive attitude

Consider the stressful nature of a customer service job—constantly dealing with complaints, negative feedback, and customer frustration. Being able to maintain a positive attitude in these situations can help service agents avoid burnout, stay motivated, maintain good performance and high productivity levels. A positive attitude is also the key to more effective customer interactions, building emotional connections with customers, and creating positive service experiences.

9. Adaptability and flexibility

No list of good customer service skills is complete without adaptability and flexibility. There is a lot of variability in the average customer support rep's daily routine. Such as different customer personalities, different problems to solve, and different support channels to manage. Therefore, adaptability and mental flexibility are critical skills as they help service reps adjust to challenging situations that can arise.

10. Time management

Since customer service agents usually have a variety of tasks and responsibilities to handle during the day, time management is one of the must-have skills for customer service agents. Time management includes smart planning, setting realistic goals, prioritizing daily activities, minimizing interruptions, and delegating tasks. These skills help service reps manage their workload effectively, meet deadlines, maintain high performance, maximize their productivity, and handle multitasking.

II
What Your Competitors Can Teach You about Customer Service

It is said that smart people learn from their mistakes, while brilliant ones learn from the mistakes of other people. The same logic can, of course, be applied to business. Further, it becomes even more important in a world where someone else's success could potentially mean your failure. By watching what our competitors are doing, we can learn a lot about what we could be doing differently to improve our own business results.

So, what is it that we can learn from others about customer service that we can use and turn into our advantage?

Problem Solving

People who contact customer support have a question or a problem that they want to see resolved. If this doesn't happen to their satisfaction, they might vent their frustration by turning to independent review sites or social media to express their dissatisfaction.

You should pay special attention to unique needs that certain types of customers have and that have gone unaddressed. It is with resolving everyone's issues that you win the most loyal customers, since they feel that your company really understands the issue and provides a unique, tailor-made solution.

Support and Respect

The whole point of customer support is to help your existing and prospective customers, while at the same time showing respect and appreciation. If you look at how your competitors deal with this issue, you might be able to learn a thing or two. Both positive and negative reviews provide valuable indications about what should and what shouldn't be done in terms of customer support.

Focus on the respect and appreciation that your competitors offer and try to give more than they do. Training agents who directly reply to customers' queries are a must, although you should also consider the services offered by a properly trained virtual receptionist. These people have undergone specialized training in communicating.

Anticipate What Your Customers Want

You can't possibly predict every single reason why people would contact you, but you should have quite a good idea about how they would like to get in touch. Your task is to anticipate all possible channels of communication that people might want to use and be present wherever people might need your help.

There is nothing wrong in keeping a close eye on your competitors' social media presence. Find out what kind of posts attract most attention and which stir up discussions. Finally, check for items such as community forums and FAQ pages, since they provide an excellent opportunity for self-service support, which is the preferred method of customer support among a great number of people.

Keep Refreshing

Just like it's important to stay fresh and innovative when it comes to your offer, the same could be said about the customer support you provide. To begin with, compare what you do with what your competitors do. If they do something you don't, or provide support in a way you don't, think about why they do it.

If you fail to see any reason, it doesn't mean it makes no sense, but don't introduce something just because someone else has it. On the other hand, if you realize that there's a good reason to start doing something differently, you should most definitely take the plunge. Just don't forget that you need to do it in such a way that your customers receive something they are unlikely to receive from anyone else. The feeling of being special is invaluable when it comes to brand loyalty.

Suppose you are Wang Hong, a salesperson at Arts & Crafts Company in Yichun, Jiangxi Province. The company has recently launched new products and planned to exhibit these items at the forthcoming China Import and Export Fair. You are going to meet customers from all over the world at the fair and are expected to give appropriate replies to their queries.

The Detailed Information of the Product		
Name	**Animal-shaped tableware**	
Item No.	NP-023	
MOQ	15 sets	
FOB Hong Kong (USD)	15–99 sets: 13.5/set	
	100–299 sets: 11.5/set	
	300–499 sets: 9.5/set	
	≥500 sets: To be negotiated	
Accessories	1 animal-shaped plate,1 circle plate, 1 bowl, 1 cup and 1 spoon	
Size	5–10 inch	
Capacity	350ml	
Types	rabbit; monkey; bear; giraffe	
Weight	1.8kg	
Safe for	microwave oven;dishwasher	
Packaging	carton box	
Lead time	1–500 sets: immediate delivery	
	≥500 sets: 10–15 days	

Now reply to the following customers' queries according to the information provided.

(1) Can I have a discount on the animal-shaped tableware?

_____

(2) What's the minimum order quantity for the animal-shaped tableware?

_____

(3) What accessories are included in the animal-shaped tableware?

_____

(4) Can animal-shaped tableware be used in microwave ovens?

_____

(5) How will the animal-shaped tableware be packed?

_____

(6) What types of animal-shaped tableware do you have?

_____

(7) What's the lead time of the animal-shaped tableware?

Ancient Chinese Wisdom

Read the following quote and answer the questions below.

Way of Heaven（天道）

Being as it is the way of nature; being true to human nature is the way to achieve self-refinement. (*The Book of Rites*)

诚者，天之道也；诚之者，人之道也。(《礼记》)

1. What truths are revealed from the above quote?

2. Sincerity and honesty are the foundation of business. How are you going to reply to customer queries sincerely and honestly?

Extended Reading

How to Respond to a Customer Request

1. Ensure that you have all information you need to respond

A good multi-channel customer support system typically provides all the information you need. This includes the name of the customer, the time when the customer request was made, related tags, etc. Make sure that your answer works to resolve a customer's issue, and review everything.

The more information you have about the customer and their problem, the better your chance is to solve it.

2. Avoid unnecessary complexity

Anything that can make your response hard to read or understand—jargon, long, complex words or sentences, fancy fonts that may not be supported by a customer's device, etc.—should be avoided to achieve the best customer outcome.

Failure to do so is likely to result in a need for further clarification. Or, in many cases, the customer would have to find out what that fancy word that you wrote them means. Clearly, this adds more work, which is the opposite of what we're trying to achieve, so make sure that the customer will understand your message without having to clarify the meanings, etc.

3. Use the language of the customer

As a general rule, the vast majority of customers use natural, conversational language when they message service teams. You have to respond in a similar manner/language they prefer to communicate with you. Besides, this helps to avoid making customers feel like they're doing work.

Reinforce your message by using positive language. This means avoiding phrases like "you need to" and "you have to" as well as words like "don't" and "won't" because they're widely perceived as negative.

Bad example:

"No, unfortunately, we can't allow you to track five orders at a time."

Good example:

"At this moment, our website allows us to track three orders at a time only, but we really appreciate you letting us know about this improvement idea. We're constantly looking for those, and we're definitely going to consider this one. Thank you for messaging us!"

4. Ask questions in a polite and professional manner

Isn't that disappointing when a customer service representative has no idea about what you're talking about but still doesn't ask you for clarification? Don't make this mistake, and make sure that your response is professional and polite.

For example, instead of asking "What did you mean by that" try "Could you please clarify what you meant by this?"

5. Follow the three S's when asking a question

Your questions will be more effective if they are:

Simple. Make them easy to understand; complex questions discourage customers from responding.

Short. Make every question as short as possible and make sure that you don't ask a lot of them; only one or two per message!

Specific. Focus on one problem in one question to avoid making them vague and difficult to understand.

6. Use formatting for important information

If your reply contains something of great importance, be sure to use bolding or underlining to get your message across. For example, this might be important information that the customer needs to remember in order to achieve their goal.

7. Always proofread

A silly mistake like a typo when you respond to a customer request makes entire customer service look amateur. So take a quick look before you hit "Send." This also applies to unfinished sentences, wrong names, and more.

(　　) 1. A good multi-channel customer support system should provides _____ .

    A. the name of the customer

B. the time when the customer request was made

C. the details of the customer requests

D. all of the above

(　　) 2. If you want to make your response easy to read or understand, you should use ＿＿

＿＿ .

A. jargon

B. long, complex words or sentences

C. clear, positive expressions

D. fancy fonts

(　　) 3. Which is NOT the three S's according to the passage?

A. Short.　　　　B. Smart.　　　　C. Simple.　　　　D. Specific.

(　　) 4. What does the passage mainly talk about?

A. Tips for replying to customer requests by face-to-face conversations.

B. Tips for replying to customer requests by answering phone calls.

C. Tips for replying to customer requests by writing a responding email.

D. Tips for replying to customer requests by asking questions.

(　　) 5. We can conclude from the passage that ＿＿＿＿＿ .

A. phrases like "you have to" as well as words like "won't" should be used when replying to customer requests

B. when a customer service representative has no idea about what the customer is talking about, he has no need to ask for clarification

C. using bolding or underlining to get your message across will make customer confused

D. a silly mistake like an unfinished sentence when responding to a customer request makes entire customer service look amateur

Write an Order Confirmation Email

Scenario

● Industry Outlook

China is committed to comprehensively improving the efficiency of resource utilization and accelerating green and low-carbon development on the premise of strictly protecting the ecological environment. The automobile industry, as the "pearl" in the crown of modern industry, is recognized as one of the most important symbols that can reflect the country's manufacturing strength.

In the past decade, the Chinese automotive industry has taken advantage of new energy vehicles and achieved great changes. The Chinese new energy vehicle industry has not only accelerated, but also become a leader in driving the electrification transformation of the global automotive industry.

● Business Task

New Era Lithium Technology Co., Ltd. is a global leader of new energy innovative technologies, committed to providing premier solutions and services for new energy applications worldwide. Communication with customers, introducing the company's products is the main channel for foreign trade enterprises to expand overseas customers.

Confirming an order is an important part of any business-customer relationship. When a company receives an order letter, it often responds with a confirmation email. Companies send this transactional email to provide the customers with detailed information about their order. It must be clear and specific about what is being confirmed or what is being changed.

Words, Phrases and Sentences

Words and phrases concerning order confirmation.

1. Translate the following words and phrases into Chinese or English.

○ **Order**

ship all orders _____

change orders _____

cancel orders _____

国际订单 _____

下订单 _____

接受订单 _____

○ **Email**

receive an email _____

send an email _____

forward the email to you _____

订单确认邮件 _____

通过电子邮件发送文档 _____

电子邮件地址 _____

○ **Payment**

terms of payment _____

payment in advance _____

pay on delivery _____

现金收付 _____

预付定金 _____

按揭付款 _____

2. Translate the following phrases into Chinese.

(1) order number _____

(2) quantity _____

(3) price (per item) _____

(4) shipping address _____

(5) delivery terms _____

(6) in/out of stock _____

(7) catalogue _____

(8) sample _____

(9) package _____

(10) item models _____

3. Translate the following phrases into English.

(1) 销售代表 _____

(2) 常年客户 _____

(3) 紧迫的事情 _____

(4) 国际品牌 _____

(5) 了解订单概况 _____

(6) 形式发票 _____

(7) 意外延误 _____

(8) 产品目录 _____

(9) 银行转账 _____

(10) 最后期限之前 _____

4. Find the words or phrases in the text with the meanings below and write them on the lines.

(1) _____ a supply of goods that is available for sale in a shop/store

(2) _____ a general description or an outline of sth.

(3) _____ a point in time by which sth. must be done

(4) _____ the skill with which sb. makes sth., especially when this affects the way it looks or works

(5) _____ a list of goods that have been sold, work that has been done etc., showing what you must pay

(6) _____ money paid for work before it has been done or money paid earlier than expected

(7) _____ a person who has been chosen to speak or vote for sb. else or on behalf of a group

(8) _____ a thing that you do to help sb.

(9) _____ transfer (cargo) from one ship, carrier, etc. to another

(10) _____ a request to make or supply goods

5. Complete the following sentences by filling in each blank with an appropriate word from the box below. Change its form if necessary.

represent	stock	fine	confirm	suppose
deadline	overview	press	transship	case

(1) We have a large _____ of imported fruit and we need to sell them quickly.

(2) We were not able to meet the _____ because of shipping delays.

(3) It is not easy to finish such _____ work which requires a good eye and a steady hand.

(4) Let's begin with the introduction part which gives an _____ of the book's contents.

(5) *David Copperfield*, an autobiographical novel, is well known as the _____ work of Charles Dickens, the greatest novelist in the Victorian period.

(6) I'm afraid I can't go with you right now, I have some _____ business to attend to.

(7) We don't have liners to China, we must _____ the good at Sydney.

(8) In this _____ , we should reject your order.

(9) You're not _____ walk on the grass.

(10) Could you please _____ your attendance at this meeting? I'm keen to find out who will be joining us.

6. Fill in the blanks with appropriate words.

(1) We are pleased to _____ （确认你方订单）which we have accepted on the terms.

(2) We are pleased to say that we have already _____ （订货单已备妥）and you may expect delivery within the next 3 days.

(3) We appreciate the business you have been able to give us and _____ （确保）you that your order will receive our most careful attention.

(4) We believe that many years of our experiences in international trade will undoubtedly _____ （满足你方要求）.

(5) We appreciate your cooperation and look forward to _____ （收到更多订单）.

7. Translate the following sentences into English.

(1) 随信附上最新的产品目录。

_____

(2) 你方 4 月 20 日订单目前在生产中。

_____

(3) 通常我们需要预付发票金额的 30%。

_____

(4) 我们保证三月第一周前交货。

_____

(5) 在这种情况下，交货时间会更长。

I
How to write an Order Confirmation Email

Order confirmation emails are one of the most valuable emails. When a customer places an order on your website, they expect to receive a purchase confirmation email. The confirmation email provides them with the reassurance that their order has been successfully placed and reminds them of their order details. A confirmation email should reply with information on price, stock, delivery and payment etc. so that the buyer can be better-informed on how their order will be processed.

Usually, a well-written and error-free email adds professionalism to your confirmation and an order confirmation email should be clear, informative, and friendly. It helps reassure the customer that their order has been successfully placed and builds trust in your business. A confirmation email should include the following information.

1. Subject Line: Use a subject line that clearly indicates the purpose of the email, such as "Order Confirmation" .

2. Greeting: Start your email with a warm and personalized greeting, addressing the customer.

3. Acknowledging the Order: Confirm the specific purchases or services such as the products and express the gratitude.

4. Order Details: Provide a clear and concise summary of the order, including the order number, date of purchase, and any relevant information such as quantities, sizes, or variations.

5. Payment Information: Confirm the payment method used and mention any payment confirmation or transaction ID.

6. Delivery Information: Specify how the customer will receive the product or service.

7. Additional Information: Include any additional information the customer may need, such as warranty details, return policy, or customer support contact information.

8. Express Appreciation: Express appreciation to the customer for choosing your business and hope for future cooperation with the client.

9. Closing: End the email with "Thank you for your order" or "We look forward to serving you" . Sign off with a professional closing, such as "Best regards" or "Sincerely. " Finally, Include your contact information, including customer support email and phone number, so the customer can reach out to you if needed.

From: davidli@123.com
To: Liu Da@y&gmail.com
Subject: hotel confirmation
Dear Mr. Liu,

Thank you for your letter dated July 23rd. We have, as requested, reserved for you: Two single rooms with breakfast for two nights from September 1st to 2nd at RMB 400 per night.

The normal check-in time is 12:00 noon, and check-out time 2:00 p.m.. As you have informed us that your flight will be arriving at 10:30 a.m. and you will be reaching the resort at 11:00 a.m., we have managed an early check-in for your convenience.

Further details of your booking are listed below.

Number of guests: 2
Room type: single, no smoking
Amenities: Free WiFi, Gym.

If there is anything additional we can do for you, please do let us know. We appreciate the opportunity to be of any help to you. We are looking forward to your visit and hope you will enjoy your stay.

Sincerely yours,
David Li
Reservation Department, West Lake Hotel

Answer the following questions.

1. What kind of letter is this?

_____

2. What did Liu Da reserve in his letter?

_____

3. How long will Liu Da stay in the hotel?

_____

Direction

Suppose you are Wang Qin, a sales representative at New Era Lithium Technology Co., Ltd.. Your company has received an order from a car company which makes an order of lithium batteries. Now you are going to write a confirmation email to Edmund Nixon, the marketing manager of the car company.

The Detailed Information of the Order	
Quantity	5,000 pieces
Description	12V 7.5ah Battery for Electric Car
Shipment	By December 15th, 2023
Mode of Transport	Ocean freight
Payment	an advance of 30% of the amount of the invoice

Now complete the confirmation email according to the information provided.

From: Wang Qin@hotmail .com
To: Edmund Nixon@hotmail .com
Subject: Order confirmation
Dear Edmund Nixon,

Thank you for (1) _____（订单）for 5,000 battery. We are happy that you made a new order for our products. We (2) _____（附上确认函）with you the quantity and the price stated in your email. As for the payment, we need (3) _____（预付发票金额的 30%）. We ensure that all the items you required are (4) _____（有库存）and you can receive your goods (5) _____（在之前）December 15,2023.

Best wishes,
Wang Qin
New Era Lithium Technology Co., Ltd.

Ancient Chinese Wisdom

Read the following quote and answer the questions below.

Good Faith（信）

Confucius said: "How can an ox-drawn wagon be pulled if it has no yoke-bar, or a horse-drawn cart be pulled if it has no collar-bar? What good is a man if he acts without good faith? " (*The Analects*)

人而无信，不知其可也。大车无輗，小车无軏，其何以行之哉？（《论语》）

(**Notes:** Integrity is known as an important traditional virtue of the Chinese nation. For an enterprise and group, it serves as an image, brand and credibility, which is a foundation for the prosperity of the enterprise.)

1. In the workplace, which is more important, integrity or ability?

_____

2. How important is integrity in business operation?

_____

Extended Reading

The Development of Orders and Future Trends

I. The Development of Orders

An order is a set of instructions to a broker to buy or sell an asset on a trader's behalf. There are multiple order types, which will affect what price the investor buys or sells at, when they will buy or sell, or whether their order will be filled or not. In the past few decades, the concept and practice of orders have undergone significant changes.

Initially, orders were primarily in paper form, with businesses and customers communicating through written agreements to confirm purchase intentions and terms. With the advancement of technology, especially e-commerce, the form of orders began to shift towards digitization. Users can now place orders through electronic devices such as computers and mobile phones on various online platforms, greatly improving the efficiency and convenience of order processing.

II. Future Development Trends of Orders

1. Intelligence: With the development of artificial intelligence and machine learning technologies, the processing of orders in the future will become more intelligent. Systems can predict users' needs based on historical data and user behavior, automatically generate and send orders, further improving the efficiency and accuracy of order processing.

2. Personalization: With consumers' increasing demand for personalized products and services, the processing of orders in the future will focus more on personalization. For example, products and services can be recommended based on users' purchase history and preferences, providing a more personalized shopping experience.

3. Contactless Service: Due to the impact of the pandemic, contactless service has become a new trend. The processing of orders in the future will place more emphasis on contactless service to reduce face-to-face interactions and enhance service safety and convenience.

4. Diversified Payment Methods: With the diversification of payment methods, the processing of orders in the future will support more payment options. In addition to traditional credit and debit card payments, it will also accommodate mobile payments, digital currency payments, and other payment methods.

5. Sustainability: With increasing environmental awareness, the processing of orders in the future will prioritize sustainability. For example, it can involve optimizing packaging materials, reducing unnecessary packaging, supporting recyclable materials, and other measures to minimize environmental impact.

Overall, the processing of orders in the future will become more intelligent, personalized, contactless, diversified, and sustainable. This will bring more convenience and innovation to both consumers and businesses.

Read the passage above and decide whether the statements are true (T) or false (F).

(   ) 1. The Initial orders were mainly in paper form.

(   ) 2. The purchasing preferences of customers will be recorded by the system and used as the basis for business orders.

(   ) 3. Environmentally friendly orders will become the trend for future orders.

(   ) 4. Face-to-face communication in transactions will continue to increase in future orders.

(   ) 5. Traditional credit card payments are considered the safest payment method.

Reference

[1] 袁洪 . 职场实用英语交际教程（初级）[M]. 北京：外语教学与研究出版社，2021.

[2]《中华思想文化术语》编委会 . 中华思想文化术语 [M]. 北京：外语教学与研究出版社，2021.

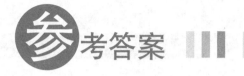

参考答案 ▐▐▐

Unit 1　Announce a Team Building Event

Words and phrases concerning team building.

1. Translate the following words and phrases into Chinese or English.

○ **Team**

加强团队精神

国家队

调查组

administrative department

mutual-aid team

team leader

○ **Announcement**

会议通知

公布结果

公告

award announcement

oral announcement

make an announcement

○ **Cooperation**

文化合作

共同努力

相互合作

strengthen cooperation

international cooperation

cooperate closely

2. Translate the following phrases into Chinese.

(1) 团建活动

(2) 建立团队目标

(3) 身体素质

(4) 目标设定

(5) 团队成员

(6) 团队目标

(7) 误解

(8) 未来的合作

(9) 旅行社

(10) 重大事件

3. Translate the following phrases into English.

(1) new staff members

(2) strengthen communication

(3) a great opportunity

(4) get to know each other

(5) the weekly meeting

(6) get better prepared

(7) general manager

(8) make a final decision

(9) keep pace with times

(10) go back to you

4. Find the words or phrases in the text with the meanings below and write them on the lines.

(1) charge

(2) further

(3) invite

(4) specialize

(5) agency

(6) detail

(7) employ

(8) strengthen

(9) opportunity

(10) announce

5. Complete the following sentences by filling in each blank with an appropriate word or phrase from the box below. Change its form if necessary.

(1) multi-function hall

(2) relaxing

(3) participation

(4) charge

(5) schedule

(6) performance

(7) split

(8) treasure

(9) reflect

(10) invited

6. Fill in the blanks with appropriate words.

(1) make an announcement

(2) great opportunity

(3) multi-function hall

(4) specializing in, in charge of

(5) live performances

7. Translate the following sentences into English.

(1) The event can build on our team spirit.

(2) In order to get to know each other better, our company has decided to organize a team-building event.

(3) There will be 5–6 members in each team.

(4) Team leaders summarize their team's performance in the end.

(5) Some gifts will be handed out to all the participants.

Task

(1) I have an announcement to make

(2) organize a team-building event for new staff

(3) the sports center

(4) some interesting activities

(5) Thanks for listening

Ancient Chinese Wisdom

略。

Extended Reading

1. D

2. A

3. A

4. A

5. A

Unit 2　Write a Hotel Reservation Email

Words and phrases concerning reservation emails.

1. Translate the following words and phrases into Chinese or English.

○ **Reserve**

预定

订座

订票

reserve a room

confirm a reservation

cancel a reservation

○ **Attend**

参加招待会

参加展销会

参加晚宴

attend a meeting

attendee

attend a seminar

○ **Confirm**

确认入住时间

订单确认邮件

确认房型

confirm an order

confirm a reservation

confirm check-out time

2. Translate the following phrases into Chinese.

(1) 房型

(2) 房价

(3) 自助早餐

(4) 持卡人

(5) 信用卡

(6) 居住时间

(7) 抵达时间

(8) 离店时间

(9) 五星级住宿设施

(10) 旅游景点

(11) 套餐

(12) 座位容量

(13) 非正式研讨会

(14) 素食套餐

(15) 预约

3. Translate the following phrases into English.

(1) check in

(2) check out

(3) single room

(4) double room

(5) twin room

(6) cross-border e-commerce

(7) annual meeting

(8) Trade Association

(9) Director of Administration Department

(10) marketing strategy

4. Find the words or phrases in the text with the meanings below and write them on the lines.

(1) cover

(2) budget

(3) gym

(4) projector

(5) access

(6) equip

(7) facility

(8) annual

(9) reserve

(10) vegetarian

5. Complete the following sentences by filling in each blank with an appropriate word or phrase from the box below. Change its form if necessary.

(1) access

(2) budget

(3) gym

(4) projector

(5) equipped

(6) cover

(7) reserve

(8) delivery

(9) payments

(10) order

6. Fill in the blanks with appropriate words.

(1) reserve

(2) arriving

(3) reply

(4) confirm

(5) requirements

7. Translate the following sentences into English.

(1) To meet your requirements, I recommend the Hill Hotel.

(2) If you have any other questions, please let me know.

(3) The meal cost is within our budget.

(4) The hotel general manager confirmed the room reservation.

(5) Please reply to confirm my reservation.

Reading

Ⅱ

1. hotel Reservation letter

2. three doulde rooms

3. ten days

Task

(1) We will hold an annual business meeting at your hotel

(2) We need a projector

(3) We have 100 attendants

(4) We need 10 double rooms and 2 single rooms

(5) confirm my reservation

Ancient Chinese Wisdom

略。

Extended Reading

1. D

2. B

3. D

4. D

5 D

Unit 3　Write a Quick Operation Guide

Words and phrases concerning operation guide.

1. Translate the following words and phrases into Chinese or English.

○ **Operation**

计算机操作

商业运营

电力驱动

operation guide

operating projector

technical operation

○ **Guide**

消费者指南

操作指南

实用指南

travel guide

user guide

guidance note

○ **Concise**

简要介绍

简编，简明的版本

简洁的设计

concise guide

concise description

conciseness principle

2. Translate the following phrases into Chinese.

(1) 用户手册

(2) 操作系统

(3) 软件安装

(4) 网络配置

(5) 投影仪屏幕

(6) 启动计算机

(7) 设置扫描仪

(8) 将路由器连接到互联网

(9) 智能家居

(10) 连接蓝牙

3. Translate the following phrases into English.

(1) brand-new meeting room

(2) quick operation guide

(3) turn on the projector

(4) concise and easy to read

(5) express…clearly

(6) shut down the projector

(7) count on me

(8) get the guide done

(9) no problem

(10) help me with this

4. Find the words or phrases in the text with the meanings below and write them on the lines.

(1) project

(2) cable

(3) observe

(4) signal

(5) lens cover

(6) electrical outlet

(7) concise

(8) procedure

(9) remain

(10) extend

5. Complete the following sentences by filling in each blank with an appropriate word or phrase from the box below. Change its form if necessary.

(1) brand-new

(2) remain

(3) cord

(4) extend

(5) procedure

(6) previous

(7) projected

(8) plug

(9) signal

(10) concise

6. Fill in the blanks with appropriate words.

(1) emergency procedures

(2) confirmation message

(3) public image

(4) plug into

(5) basic requirement

7. Translate the following sentences into English.

(1) If you need to turn off the projector, please press the power button on the remote control twice in a row.

(2) I'll have to change the plug on my hairdryer.

(3) The power light flashes red or green as the system starts up.

(4) Press these two keys to switch between documents on screen.

(5) Warning! Continuing the operation may cause data loss.

Task

(1) Insert paper
(2) Connect the power cord
(3) power button
(4) the printer drivers
(5) the power lamp lights

Ancient Chinese Wisdom

略。

Extended Reading

1. A
2. A
3. C
4. B
5. B

Unit 4   Reply to Technical Enquiries

Words and phrases concerning technical enquiries.

1. Translate the following words and phrases into Chinese or English.

○ **Reply**

匿名回复

做出回复

收到回复

reply card

reply to an e-mail

thoughtful reply

○ **Technical**

技术服务

技术支持

技巧训练

technical issues

information technology

wireless technology

○ **Enquiry**

技术咨询

免费查询服务

查询系统

Enquiry Software

Customers' enquiries

Enquiry and Feedback

2. Translate the following phrases into Chinese.

(1) 背景查询

(2) 技术专家

(3) 触屏手机

(4) 型号

(5) 手机信号

(6) 技术进步

(7) 技术错误

(8) 秘书服务

(9) 一般性询问

(10) 可充电电池

3. Translate the following phrases into English.

(1) customer care centre

(2) technical problem

(3) smart phone

(4) standby time

(5) phone model number

(6) view websites

(7) regardless of

(8) Model Ⅳ

(9) deal with problems

(10) call them back

4. Find the words or phrases in the text with the meanings below and write them on the lines.

(1) bright

(2) clear

(3) adviser

(4) improper

(5) update

(6) battery

(7) drain

(8) enquiry

(9) professional

(10) normal

5. Complete the following sentences by filling in each blank with an appropriate word or phrase from the box below. Change its form if necessary.

(1) brightness

(2) examination

(3) unstable

(4) professional

(5) sensible

(6) notify

(7) drained

(8) improper

(9) updating

(10) Normal

6. Fill in the blanks with appropriate words.

(1) make an appointment

(2) explain the technical principles

(3) follow the industry standards

(4) encounter network connectivity issues

(5) repair your mobile phone

7. Translate the following sentences into English.

(1) The phone signal here is poor.

(2) Thanks for your understanding, and you are really thoughtful.

(3) As much as I'd love to help any further questions of our products.

(4) The printer may be jammed because the paper is damp.

(5) Your machine may need to be returned to the factory for further examination.

Task

(1) thanks for calling

(2) the monitor went black

(3) your computer might have a virus

(4) you run an antivirus program

(5) if the problem has been solved

Ancient Chinese Wisdom

略。

Extended Reading

1. C

2. A

3. B

4. D

5. A

Unit 5   Make a Business Trip Itinerary

Words and phrases concerning making a business trip itinerary.

1. Translate the following words and phrases into Chinese or English.

○ **Launch**

新书发布会

参加新书发布会

发布日期

product launch

launch the latest novel

launch a satellite

○ **Arrange**

安排会面

安排一辆车

安排新书发布会

arrange a meeting

arrange an employee

arrange a business trip

○ **Itinerary**

商务行程

在行程上

制定行程

change the itinerary

show the manager the intermarry

itinerary map

2. Translate the following phrases into Chinese.

(1) 争分夺秒

(2) 预订满了

(3) 推迟来访

(4) 顾问委员会

(5) 紧凑的行程

(6) 跟着行程路线走

(7) 出发日期

(8) 在他抵达时

(9) 起草一份商务行程安排

(10) 作比较

3. Translate the following phrases into English.

(1) publishing house

(2) launch a new book

(3) forward an e-mail

(4) give a speech

(5) make an itinerary

(6) direct flight

(7) leave the afternoon free

(8) draft the itinerary

(9) preferred travel dates

(10) deeply impressed

4. Find the words or phrases in the text with the meanings below and write them on the lines.

(1) comparison

(2) launch

(3) departure

(4) promote

(5) impress

(6) draft

(7) publish

(8) award-winning

(9) schedule

(10) vegetarian

5. Complete the following sentences by filling in each blank with an appropriate word or phrase from the box below. Change its form if necessary.

(1) drafted

(2) promote

(3) launched

(4) departure

(5) impressed

(6) comparison

(7) promoted

(8) impression

(9) compare

(10) depart

6. Fill in the blanks with appropriate words.

(1) arrange accommodation

(2) forward his e-mail to you

(3) go sightseeing

(4) get in touch

(5) make an itinerary

7. Translate the following sentences into English.

(1) I hope this plan works for you.

(2) What's the departure and arrival time?

(3) We plan to hold a book launch on July 15th at Donghu Hotel.

(4) John is going to pick up Professor Lee at the airport tomorrow.

(5) I'm quite delighted to give a speech at the event.

Task

Date	Time	Event	Detail
July 24th	2 p.m.	Arrive at Yichun Mingyueshan Airport; Check in at Donghu Hotel	CZ 3384 12:25 p.m.(Guangzhou)– 2:00 p.m.(Yichun)
July 25th	8 a.m.	Attend the conference	At Conference Hall 1, Donghu Hotel
	2 p.m.	Give a speech	
July 26th	8:30 a.m.	Attend 2 seminars with the delegation from New Era Lithium Technology Co., Ltd.	At Conference Hall 3, Donghu Hotel
	2:10 p.m.	Go to Wentang Town to experience hot spring bath	
July 27th	9 a.m.	Go hiking at Mingyue Mountain; Have a cable car ride going down the mountain	By car; Picked up by Mr.Wang from the hotel
	5 p.m.	Visit the Gulou night market; Have dinner at a local Yichun food restaurant	Transfer by car
July 28th	7:30 p.m.	Check out of Donghu Hotel; Depart from Yichun Mingyueshan Airport	CZ6672 9:00 a.m.(Yichun)– 11:55 a.m.(Guangzhou)

Ancient Chinese Wisdom

略。

Extended Reading

1. F

2. F

3. F

4. T

5. F

6. F

7. T

Unit 6   Receive a Business Client

Words and phrases concerning receiving a business client.

1. Translate the following words and phrases into Chinese or English.

○ **Develop**

开发产品

冲洗照片

发展关系

develop business

develop photos

develop habits

○ **Receive**

接待商务客户

收到礼物

收到信号

receive orders

receive guests

receive blame

○ **Found**

创办公司

建立在信任的基础上

有充分根据的

found a football club

be founded on mutual respect

found an investment institution

2. Translate the following phrases into Chinese.

(1) 接待一位重要的客户

(2) 安排会面

(3) 财政困难

(4) 紧凑的行程

(5) 欢迎宴会

(6) 证券公司

(7) 发展业务关系

(8) 确认客户身份

(9) 给人留下好印象

(10) 闲谈

3. Translate the following phrases into English.

(1) vice president

(2) financial product

(3) give him a hand

(4) financial department

(5) arrange for a car

(6) give you a hand

(7) hold a half share

(8) be mistaken about someone

(9) all the year round

(10) a nice stay

4. Find the words or phrases in the text with the meanings below and write them on the lines.

(1) develop

(2) stand

(3) serious

(4) refuse

(5) typical

(6) intelligent

(7) communicate

(8) share

(9) energetic

(10) preparation

5. Complete the following sentences by filling in each blank with an appropriate word

(1) intelligent

(2) refused

(3) typical

(4) serious

(5) developing

(6) stand

(7) developing

(8) refuse

(9) typical

(10) serious

6. Fill in the blanks with appropriate words.

(1) gets involved in

(2) are mistaken about

(3) all the year round

(4) would be a good choice

(5) arrange an appointment

(6) start the communication

7. Translate the following sentences into English.

(1) We are going to take you to the hotel for a rest.

(2) We sincerely hope Mr. Brian will have a nice stay in Beijing.

(3) We are going to attend two meetings and a seminar with the mayor.

(4) Generally speaking, the weather in Guangzhou is mild all the year round.

(5) Speaking of local food, he is an expert about it!

Task

(1) What's your first impression about Guangzhou

(2) Do you find the weather here agreeable

(3) How was your flight

(4) We are heading for the hotel now

(5) you will attend a seminar with our marketing team

Ancient Chinese Wisdom

略。

Extended Reading

1. F

2. F

3. T

4. F

5. T

6. F

Unit 7　Write a Market Research Report

Words and phrases concerning writing a market research report.

1. Translate the following words and phrases into Chinese or English.

○ **Market**

农产品市场

当地市场

在市场上

global market

market size

market share

○ **Research**

市场调研

研究项目

调查

research paper

conduct a research

medical research

○ **Interview**

采访一位顾客

街头采访

要求采访

random interview

have an interview with somebody

exclusive interview

2.Translate the following phrases into Chinese.

(1) 发展趋势

(2) 占……

(3) 不含脂肪

(4) 得出结论

(5) 开展市场调研

(6) 增长

(7) 国内市场

(8) 促销特卖

(9) 就业市场

(10) 就业面试

3. Translate the phrases into English.

(1) weekly meeting

(2) market research

(3) the latest product

(4) energy drinks

(5) offer coupons

(6) vending machine

(7) blue collar

(8) report to someone

(9) work out

(10) have more promotion

4. Find the words in the text with the meanings below and write them on the lines.

(1) convenience store

(2) develop

(3) advertise

(4) platform

(5) white collar

(6) packaging

(7) vending machine

(8) discount

(9) coupon

(10) investigate

5. Complete the following sentences by filling in each blank with an appropriate word from the box below. Change its form if necessary.

(1) effectively

(2) presented

(3) interviewed

(4) frequency

(5) feature

(6) channel

(7) frequent

(8) channels

(9) featured

(10) presentation

6. Fill in the blanks with appropriate words.

(1) making a plan

(2) write a report

(3) surf the Internet

(4) works out

(5) detailed information

7. Translate the following sentences into English.

(1) I tried your new energy drink yesterday, and it tastes great!

(2) To be honest, I prefer to buy energy drinks in convenience stores.

(3) Please write a market research and hand it to the manager by this Friday.

(4) You should advertise the new product through more channels.

(5) Energy drinks don't appeal to me.

Task

	A Market Research Report on the Newly-developed New Energy Car
Introduction	The company has developed a new type of energy car, and plans to put it into market next year
Aim	In order to know people's intention of buying this new type of car and make marketing strategies, we have conducted a market research
Results	We handed out 3,000 copies of questionnaire to target customers. The data shows that 32% of the interviewees think price is an important factor in their decision to purchase. 19% of the interviewees think the appearance of the car is what really matters to them. Another 49% of the interviewees take function as their top priority when purchasing a car
Conclusions	The new type of new energy car produced in our company meets the expectations of most interviewees. As a result, we estimate that the car will be popular after being put into market and the sales volume will increase steadily

Ancient Chinese Wisdom

略。

Extended Reading

1. F

2. F

3. T

4. F

5. T

Unit 8 Introduce a New Product

Words and phrases concerning new product.

1. Translate the following words and phrases into Chinese or English.

○ **Product**

介绍一款新产品

产品介绍

销售产品

promote product

product strategy

production position

○ **Customer**

目标客户

客户需求

长期客户

attract customer

prospective customer

customer satisfaction

○ **Introduction**

产品介绍

采用新设计

引入新概念

introduction speech

organize a production introduction

introduce foreign capital

2. Translate the following phrases into Chinese.

(1) 产品特征

(2) 优势

(3) 目标客户

(4) 价格策略

(5) 市场调查

(6) 客户关注

(7) 推出产品

(8) 产品目录

(9) 售后服务

(10) 卖点

(11) 客户需求

(12) 特价（商品）

(13) 产品介绍

(14) 产品特点

(15) 满足顾客的需求

3. Translate the following phrases into English.

(1) travel package

(2) travel agency

(3) meet sb's needs/satisfy sb's needs

(4) destination

(5) Group travel

(6) focus on sb's needs

(7) cover expense

(8) HR manager

(9) tourist site

(10) relatively low

4. Find the words or phrases in the text with the meanings below and write them on the lines.

(1) airfare

(2) recommendation

(3) concern

(4) selling point

(5) full board

(6) exclusion

(7) trip

(8) introduce

(9) expect

(10) design

5. Complete the following sentences by filling in each blank with an appropriate word or phrase from the box below. Change its form if necessary.

(1) round-trip

(2) concern

(3) tourist sites

(4) airfare

(5) airport transfer

(6) full board

(7) exclusion

(8) selling point

(9) check-in

(10) Relatively

6. Fill in the blanks with appropriate words.

(1) discount

(2) consider

(3) hesitate

(4) looking for

(5) provide

7. Translate the following sentences into English.

(1) Our product can solve your problem perfectly.

(2) Our travel package can provide you with a satisfying and unforgettable experience.

(3) Tourist groups with more than 20 people enjoy a 20% discount.

(4) At the same time, we also provide full board services.

(5) If you are interested in our package, please feel free to contact us.

Task

略。

Ancient Chinese Wisdom

略。

Extended Reading

1. B

2. A

3. D

4. C

5. A

Unit 9   Reply to Customer Queries

Words and phrases concerning reply to customer queries.

1. Translate the following words and phrases into Chinese or English.

○ **Price**

市场价

批发价

零售价

reduce price

sale price

Tax-Paid Price (TTP)

○ **Brand**

占市场最大份额的品牌，名牌

品牌选择

（消费者）对品牌的忠实度

brand image

brand-new

brand awareness

○ **Delivery**

即时交货

货到付款

款到发货

free delivery

delivery date

delivery cycle

2. Translate the following phrases into Chinese.

(1) 包装

(2) 二维码

(3) 展示柜

(4) 出公告，做广告

(5) 小册子

(6) 定制、定做

(7) 保证，保单

(8) 特许经销权、特许经销

(9) 售后服务

(10) 平均订单价值

3. Translate the following phrases into English.

(1) arts & crafts company

(2) Import and Export Fair

(3) potential customer

(4) business exhibition

(5) product catalogue

(6) lead time

(7) MOQ (minimum order quantity)

(8) FOB (free on board)

(9) hot sale item

(10) final confirmation

4. Find the words or phrases in the text with the meanings below and write them on the lines.

(1) fair

(2) exhibit

(3) query

(4) discount

(5) exceed

(6) delivery

(7) range

(8) potential

(9) colleague

(10) estimate

5. Complete the following sentences by filling in each blank with an appropriate word or phrase from the box below. Change its form if necessary.

(1) estimated

(2) range

(3) immediately

(4) queries

(5) handle

(6) exceeded

(7) colleagues

(8) potential

(9) negotiating

(10) catalogue

6. Fill in the blanks with appropriate words.

(1) deliveries

(2) packed

(3) reduce

(4) damage in transit

(5) Strict quality control

7. Translate the following sentences into English.

(1) The goods are ready for immediate delivery.

(2) The packaging shall be at the seller's option.

(3) All the offers are subject to our final confirmation.

(4) The discount depends on the order size.

(5) We may give a 30% discount if you order more than 500 pieces.

Task

(1) Yes. If you order more than 500 sets, we will give you a discount.

(2) The minimum order quality is 15 sets.

(3) It includes 1 animal-shaped plate,1 circle plate, 1 bowl, 1 cup and 1 spoon.

(4) Yes, it can.

(5) It will be packed in carton boxes.

(6) We have rabbit,monkey,bear and giraffe.

(7) It's being prepared for immediate delivery, but it's estimated to be 10–15 days for the production of more than 500 sets.

Ancient Chinese Wisdom

略。

Extended Reading

1. D

2. C

3. B

4. C

5. D

Unit 10 Write an Order Confirmation Email

Words and phrases concerning order confirmation.

1. Translate the following words and phrases into Chinese or English.

○ **Order**

运输所有的订单

更换订单

取消订单

international orders

place an order

accept an order

○ **Email**

收到邮件

发送邮件

转发电子邮件

order confirmation order

email the documents

email address

○ **Payment**

支付方式

预付货款

货到付款

payment in cash

a down payment

mortgage payments

2. Translate the following phrases into Chinese.

(1) 订单号

(2) 数量

(3) 价格

(4) 寄送地址

(5) 发货条款

(6) 有 / 无库存

(7) 产品目录

(8) 样品

(9) 包装

(10) 货物型号

3. Translate the following phrases into English.

(1) a sales representative

(2) a regular client

(3) a pressing matter

(4) international brand

(5) get an overview of her order

(6) proforma invoice

(7) unexpected delay

(8) product catalogue

(9) bank transfer

(10) ahead of the deadline

4. Find the words or phrases in the text with the meanings below and write them on the lines.

(1) stock

(2) overview

(3) deadline

(4) workmanship

(5) invoice

(6) advance

(7) representative

(8) favour

(9) transship

(10) order

5. Complete the following sentences by filling in each blank with an appropriate word from the box below. Change its form if necessary.

(1) Stock

(2) deadline

(3) fine

(4) overview

(5) representative

(6) pressing

(7) transship

(8) case

(9) supposed to

(10) confirm

6. Fill in the blanks with appropriate words.

(1) confirm your order

(2) made up your order

(3) assure

(4) meet your requirement

(5) receiving your further orders

7. Translate the following sentences into English.

(1) The latest category is enclosed.

(2) Your order of April 20th is currently in production.

(3) Normally, we need to prepay 30% of the invoice amount.

(4) We assure that we will delivery the goods by the first week of March.

(5) In this case, the delivery will take longer.

Reading

Ⅱ

1. hotel confirmation letter

2. Two single rooms

3. Two days

Task

(1) your order

(2) enclose our sales confirmation

(3) an advance of 30% of the amount of the invoice

(4) in stock

(5) by

Ancient Chinese Wisdom

略。

Extended Reading

1. T

2. T

3. T

4. F

5. F